T5-CVH-115

LIFE WITH OL' MIKE

Wit & Wisdom on Life, Love and Happiness

Mike Oatman

HAWK PUBLISHING : TULSA

Copyright © 2004 by Mike Oatman

All rights reserved under International and Pan-American Copyright Conventions. No part of this book may be reproduced, stored in a retrieval system or transmitted in any form by an electronic, mechanical, photocopying, recording means or otherwise, without prior written permission of the author.

Published in the United States by:HAWK Publishing Group

HAWK and colophon are trademarks belonging to the HAWK Publishing Group.

Printed in the United States of America

LIBRARY OF CONGRESS CATALOGING IN PUBLICATION DATA
Oatman, Mike

  Life with Ol' Mike : wit & wisdom on life, love & happiness / Mike Oatman.

      p. cm.
      ISBN 1-930709-47-1 (alk. paper)

  1. Oatman, Mike.—Wisdom. 2. Oatman family. 3. Conduct of life—Quotations, maxims, etc. 4. Social Values—United States—Quotations, maxims, etc. 5. Meditations. I. Title.

2003

COVER AND BOOK DESIGN: Carl Brune

HAWK Publishing Group
7107 South Yale, # 345
Tulsa OK 74136
918 492 3677

www.hawkpub.com

To Pegi

You picked me up when I was broken, dusted me off and made me realize that life is still worth living, and that it's still possible to live and love, even after an unspeakable loss.

Ol' Mike

The first 60 years of our Dad's life would make a great book.

He was born in the small West Texas town of Marfa in 1939. His father died in a trucking accident before he ever knew him. His mother was a classical musician and gifted painter, but struggled with menial jobs to help support the family. She remarried a second time, only to have that husband killed in World War II. Finally, she met Arthur Oatman and he adopted Dad, his brother and their two sisters.

By the age of fourteen "Ol' Mike," as he was already known, started a western swing band that quickly became the number one dance band in Southwest Texas. When he was just seventeen he wrote a song that was recorded by Frankie Lane on his "Rawhide" album. He attended a year of college at Texas Western where he didn't receive a degree, but he did meet our mom, Barbara Jane Cram.

He accepted a job at El Paso Radio station KHEY in 1959, and quickly worked his way up to host of the morning show, program director, and sales manager. Five years later, he responded to an ad in an industry newspaper for a job at KFDI in Wichita, Kansas. By shaking hands with Mike Lynch, he formed a partnership that would last nearly forty years.

In 1965, he and Mike Lynch bought KFDI which at the time had an annual revenue of $110,000. Over the next thirty-five years, they built Great Empire Broadcasting into a fourteen station, five state operation with annual revenues of over $15 million dollars. During those thirty-five years he also served as president of the Country Radio Broadcasters, president of the Wichita Chamber of Commerce, worked on numerous other community boards, hosted a daytime TV show, was inducted into the Country Music DJ Hall of Fame, continued to do his daily morning radio show, and served as CEO of Great Empire Broadcasting. His days started with a wake up call from the radio station at 4:45 in the morning, and ended when he got home around seven that night. Our dad was a leader in broadcasting, country music, and his community. He was the most driven, focused, fair, and consistent person who most people ever knew.

In 1999, he and Mike Lynch sold Great Empire Broadcasting for $95.9 million dollars. Of the total, over $30 million dollars was given to various employees in return for their loyalty, longevity, and service. This "rags-toriches" story of a self-made man who lived the American dream would make a great book, but, this book is about what happened next.

He spent most of his first year of retirement at Mom's hospital bedside, twelve hours a day, seven days a week until she took her last breath on May 10, 2000. After selling his company and losing Mom, Dad began to see life through a whole new set of eyes. Suddenly, he grasped the importance of all the things that he had been too busy to notice before. In December, 2000, he began writing a weekly column for the Wichita Eagle, reflecting his deepest thoughts during his last two years. Like many men of his generation, Dad had a hard time verbalizing his emotions. But in these columns he eloquently wrote of his feelings about family, friends, and all the important things in life.

Mike Oatman left a large legacy in the world of broadcasting, business, and his community. But for our family, his greatest legacies are the heartfelt emotions that are written in this book.

MELISSA, ANDY AND RICHARD OATMAN

Index of Columns

The Most Important Job   1
JUNE 1993

Selling My Life   3
OCTOBER 1998

Heartache Is Soothed by Christmases Past   5
DECEMBER 28, 2000

Angels Can Turn Up in Some of the Unlikeliest Places   9
FEBRUARY 15, 2001

Joe Frank Ferguson's Passing Leaves a Great Big Hole in Country Music   11
MARCH 15, 2001

What's a Vacation Without a Little Adventure?   13
MARCH 29, 2001

Thinking of Buying an RV? Ol' Mike Can Help You   15
APRIL 5, 2001

Cancer That Was Once Beaten Rears Its Ugly Head Again   17
APRIL 19, 2001

A Little Time with the Grandkids Renews a Weary Soul   19
APRIL 26, 2001

Things Would Be Different If I Had a Second Chance   21
MAY 3, 2001

Readers Give Ol' Mike a Humbling Lesson in Kindness Shared   23
MAY 17, 2001

With Cancer Surgery Over, Each Day Is Full of Thanks   25
JUNE 14, 2001

Family Pool Is Where Memories Are Enshrined   27
JUNE 21, 2001

Grudges Aren't Worth the Price We Pay to Carry Them   29
JULY 5, 2001

Death Takes a Gentleman and a Genius of Country Music   31
JULY 12, 2001

Another Health Concern Intrudes on Everyday Life   33
AUGUST 2, 2001

We Could Learn a Few Valuable Lessons from Our Canine Friends   35
AUGUST 16, 2001

You Mold the Clay That Is a Child's Soul   37
AUGUST 23, 2001

You Choose the Attitude That You Carry through Life   39
SEPTEMBER 6, 2001

Those Who Attacked Us Deserve Swift, Sure Justice   41
SEPTEMBER 27, 2001

Let's Hope That, This Time, Patriotism Stays in Vogue   43
OCTOBER 25, 2001

TV News Could Learn a Lot from Ernie Pyle   45
NOVEMBER 1, 2001

We Can't Let Fear Warp the Way We See Others   47
NOVEMBER 8, 2001

Life, Love, Family, Friends: Give Thanks for Them All   49
NOVEMBER 22, 2001

When You Look Like a Cue Ball, You Learn All About Humility   51
NOVEMBER 29, 2001

If There's Radio in Heaven, Willie Wheelchair's on It   53
DECEMBER 13, 2001

Imagine If Santa Claus Caught the Corporate Urge to Merge   55
DECEMBER 27, 2001

Battling Cancer Can Make You Appreciate Good Health   57
JANUARY 3, 2002

Uncle Sam's Charity Is Well-Intentioned but Misplaced   59
JANUARY 17, 2002

Golf Addict Confesses Ease with Affliction   61
JANUARY 31, 2002

Lonely Heart Waits for a Loving Home   63
FEBRUARY 21, 2002

Some Things Just Get Mike's Nanny Goat 65
FEBRUARY 28, 2002

Sales People Make the World Go Around 67
MARCH 7, 2002

Power Is Not in the Hands of Everyone 69
MARCH 21, 2002

Reflections, Forecasts of the Seasons of Our Lives 71
APRIL 4, 2002

Rude Folks Reflect Their Poor Upbringing 73
APRIL 18, 2002

Health, Friends and Memory Are Temporary 75
APRIL 25, 2002

Recalling the Sweet Music of Childhood 77
MAY 9, 2002

The Real Treasures in Life Are Found with the Heart 79
MAY 23, 2002

The World Would Be Better Off without Ties 81
MAY 30, 2002

I Wish I Had Said All This to My Father 83
JUNE 13, 2002

Late in Life Dad Learns Lesson in Fatherhood 85
JUNE 27, 2002

Our Own Greed Fueled an Economic Downfall 87
JULY 11, 2002

Visit with 'Home Folks' Teaches a Life Lesson 89
JULY 18, 2002

It's Time for Airlines to Think About Consumers 91
JULY 25, 2002

Country Music Needs to Get Back to Its Roots 93
AUGUST 8, 2002

Enthusiasm Can Unlock the Door to the Good Life 95
AUGUST 15, 2002

The World Is Full of Things That Make Me Nervous   97
AUGUST 22, 2002

Shared Grief of September 11th Changed Us, United Us   99
SEPTEMBER 5, 2002

Grandparents Hold a Store of Knowledge to Cherish   101
SEPTEMBER 12, 2002

Here's to America's Truckers   103
SEPTEMBER 19, 2002

No Matter How Much We Own, We're Renters   105
SEPTEMBER 26, 2002

Wichita Exec Latest Victim of Corporate Inhumanity   107
OCTOBER 3, 2002

It's Never Too Late to Reunite with Estranged Parents   109
OCTOBER 17, 2002

An Ode to a Trusted Companion Long Gone   111
OCTOBER 24, 2002

Dad Feels Helpless as His Youngest Heads to KC   113
OCTOBER 31, 2002

More Might Run for Office If They Knew How   115
NOVEMBER 7, 2002

We Could Learn Plenty from Elderly, If We'd Listen   117
NOVEMBER 21, 2002

Jack Jonas' Vision Was Dignity for the Disabled   119
DECEMBER 5, 2002

Ol' Mike's Holiday Joy Is Clouded by More Bad Health News   121
JANUARY 9, 2003

Ol' Mike Offers a Prayer for All in the New Year   123
JANUARY 2, 2003

Afterword   125

Wit & Wisdom on Life, Love and Happiness

The Most Important Job

JUNE 1993 : "Do you ever wish you'd married one of those women with a career?" she asked out of the clear one evening.

"Whatever do you mean?" I asked, barely glancing up from the paper, but trying to act like I was all ears.

"Oh, you know . . . one of those women who's out there . . . doing important things like managing and running things and being, you know, important!"

"Why, dear," sez I, on alert now, knowing full well that this was one of those questions calling for an answer reeking industrial-strength diplomacy and tact . . . one of those innocent-sounding female questions which, if answered without proper thought and care, could result in a landslide of hurt feelings and a long evening of contriteness from yours truly. "You know that I wouldn't trade you for ten other women, or even for a Gibson five-string banjo, for that matter! How could you even think of such a thing?"

"Oh, you know.. . . you're so important . . . you're out there every day with important people, having meetings and hobnobbing with really famous people who do important things. And then you come home to me and all I've done is clean house, fix dinner, baby-sit and chase the dogs out of the flower beds. I mean, I wouldn't blame you if you didn't find that very exciting. I mean, what's important about that?"

Luckily the phone rang.

Saved by the bell.

By the time the phone conversation was over the subject was changed and she had forgotten that I still hadn't given an answer.

She forgot, but I didn't.

The more I thought about her question, the more I knew it was important for me to answer it with the right words, Words, that would once and for all bring her the reassurance she was seeking. In true *that's-what-I-should've-said* fashion, I formulated my answer. When she asks again, I'll tell her this:

Not important?

That's like saying the sun isn't important to the earth or the stars aren't important to the sky! Comparing my job with your job is like comparing a breeze with a hurricane. My job is like Trivial Pursuit, played for the moment, and yours is like the game of Life, played for eternity.

I've spent my time making decisions, the outcome of which will little be remembered beyond my career life . . . you've spent your time making little souls who will live on beyond both our lifetimes. While I labored in control rooms and boardrooms, raising big issues of little importance, you labored in the hospital rooms, living rooms and kitchens, raising little people to become big people. When I was wiping away the competition and impressing customers with my cleverness, you were there wiping noses and bottoms and impressing little minds with the fact that someone loved them and cared for them.

I was making impressions for the moment . . . you were making impressions for the ages, I flailed away gathering a living for the family, and you steadfastly made sure there was a family to make a living for.

Not important?

My dear, when whoever keeps tabs on this earthly life tallies up, it will be clear to all who was more important. The record will show that there was in our family unit an all-powerful center which radiated a tender strength and all encompassing love that nurtured and fueled us all to perform our tasks. That was your job. Like a mother bird, you gave wings to our young and gently nudged them out of the nest to fly, after carefully preparing them for the wind and storms around them. That was your job.

And now you want to know if I regret not having someone who is 'important.' If you, and what you do, is not important, then neither is the air that we breathe or the food that we eat or the ground that we walk upon. Right now I can't think of a single person who's concerned with my 'pronouncements,' but I can think of three kids, three grandchildren, four parents, a son-in-law, an ex-daughter-in-law, a would-be-daughter-in-law, several dozen friends, three dogs, a cat and one slightly worn ol' husband who considers you to be the sweetest, kindest and most considerate person they've ever encountered.

Your job is being the center of our universe. I'd say that is important.

Wouldn't you?

IT'S ALL YOURS, JUST DON'T MESS WITH the TUNING, TREAT IT WITH RESPECT and for CRYING OUT LOUD, GET a COWBOY HAT!

(Reprinted from The Wichita Eagle)

Selling My Life

OCTOBER 1998 : My hand trembled as I reached for the pen to sign on the dotted line.

Inside a voice was saying, "I shouldn't." There was another voice, though, saying, "What a great deal! Do it!"

You see, I was selling my life. Here were these people from up North, eagerly awaiting the signature that would make them owners of the stock-and hence, the future-of Great Empire Broadcasting.

I had guided the sale from May forward on the premise that the offer was too good to turn down. And in fact, it was. There comes a time in every business when harvesting that which you have worked for is important. As the chief executive officer of Great Empire Broadcasting, my fiducial duty to our stockholder employees and the other stockholders in the company dictated that we accept this offer. I believe today that I would be derelict in my duties had I not accepted the offer, or at least strongly considered it. From a business standpoint, it was a whale of a deal. To do this business, though, I had to take my emotions and put them in a box and stick them somewhere so they couldn't get out until it was too late. Emotions would have kept me from making a good decision.

You see, I always thought that I would live forever. I always thought that I would be getting up in the morning and doing Ol' Mike's Morning Show, functioning with KFDI and doing the other business that I do with the rest of the radio stations-forever!

Health reasons—both with Mike Lynch and my wife, Janie, and to some degree myself at the beginning of the year—were kind of a wake up call that "forever" might not be quite as long as it always had seemed to me in the past.

Another shocking thing that happened

along the way—I caught a glimpse of myself in a picture, and for an instant, I didn't recognize me. *Who is that old, gray-headed, fat guy? That's not me!* I thought. *I'm a young guy!* Only hard-headed thinking and realization brought me to accept the truth. That old, gray-headed, fat-guy was me. And the birthday rushing at me in September, making me 59, brought home the reality.

This, indeed was a great offer. It was great because:

A) The price offered was more than fair and might not be obtainable under the best of scenarios for the next five or ten years of operation.

B) Janie's sweet voice gently chiding me to slow down and spend some time with her was underscored by the doctor's reports of her medical condition that will make "all those things we planned to do someday" a little more tenuous. Still doable, but tenuous.

C) Mike Lynch, my partner of all these 34 years, never once suggested that the only way to regain his lifelong investment was to sell to some outside party. Instead, he chose to sell to the employees. We would need another 10 years, under the best of circumstances, to get all of his wealth out of the operation. And in doing that, we would be strained in terms of the ability to grow and compete effectively. He had the opportunity, with this sale, to get his wealth back in one fell swoop while he still had time to enjoy and spend it.

D) Certainly important to us are employee stockholders. People we have given stock to over the years of their diligent service to the company, would be instantly secure.

For all these reasons, while my hand trembled, I went ahead and signed the agreement that sealed the fate of two-thirds of my life.

As I reflect on it today, still securing that box of emotions and afraid to reach into and examine it (I'm postponing that as long as I can), it was a home run by anybody's measurement!

As a listener, I don't think you'll notice anything different except that you won't have me to kick around anymore in the morning. You'll still hear all the top "Ranch Hands" you've come to know, love and appreciate. And I might even pop up once in a while, in some form. Maybe just selling something or reading a poem or two, but it's likely that I'll be there.

As life moves forward, someone, somewhere, will look back on this and call it a good and timely thing. As for me, when I finally get around to dealing with those emotions that I've stuck in that box in the closet where they can't interfere with good, plain-old horse sense, I hope they'll be kind. The world will spin on without Ol' Mike's Morning Show, and I suspect that I'll spin on without it, too, as Janie and I try to recapture those things that a far-too-busy youth allowed us to miss together.

I hate the word "retirement." I prefer the word "realignment."

I'll let you know how it's working.

Heartache Is Soothed by Christmases Past

DECEMBER 28, 2000 : I've dreaded the coming of Christmas this year. You see, it will be the first in 40 years without the presence of my beloved Janie. Her passing on May 10th left a void that is indescribable, and Christmas will only serve to remind the kids and me that she is gone.

Christmas was Janie's time. She decorated the house with her ceramic creations: little mice with sweet smiles painted on their faces, Santa and Mrs. Santa, and little elves busily involved in crafting gifts for little ceramic bunnies and children.

She decorated the tree with ornaments she'd collected, while I watched in wonder that she could find so much energy and produce so many wonderful things.

She cajoled me incessantly until at last I would hang those god-awful snarled lights on our trees outside. She purchased, addressed and mailed all the Christmas cards to our friends and relatives. She knew the desires of all the grandkids, and our children and our children's spouses, and conspired with each to acquire the gifts at the top of their "wish" lists.

She shopped, wrapped, decorated, baked, worried, "tizzied," as we used to say, until Christmas was letter perfect.

Not trusting me totally (ever since the year I bought her a gold lamé pantsuit) to know HER desires, she always provided me with a list of things that she would deem desirable, with sizes, colors, and sources clearly marked, so that even I, in my ineptness, could not make a mistake.

On Christmas Eve, when we'd open the presents, she'd take her place in front of the fire and manage the openings, leaving hers until last, and carefully directing the kids and grandkids so that they got the most out of the surprises awaiting them. Her chuckle and laughter was our Christmas music as this annual custom unfolded.

She would be up many times during the night carefully arranging the gifts to be discovered by the young ones, and checking on Christmas dinner, already being prepared by her loving hands.

Only after the sound of children playing with newfound toys had faded and the young families had loaded the gifts and headed for home on Christmas day, the wrappings gathered and placed in the trash, would she relax. She would study and organize her own gifts, content, I believe, in the knowledge that once again she had produced a memorable Christmas for those for whom she lived.

How could Christmas ever be happy again? How could we find meaning and celebrate with our Christmas angel gone from our midst?

All week I tried reminding myself that we are not alone, that many families are missing loved ones and experiencing the same feelings. I resolved to be strong so the little ones would not detect my sorrow and thus have their happiness spoiled.

But everything reminded me of her absence. The decorations placed by my son Richard's mother-in-law, the Christmas cards and gifts from relatives, the Christmas

CHRISTMAS 1996

carols filling the airwaves, the ads in the mail and newspapers—to be honest, I nearly drowned in self-pity and the overwhelming sense of despair. I wanted to bolt! To just leave, to disappear until the season was over. At last I understood those inevitable stories of holiday depression that always appear around this time of year. Ah, yes. I understood. I was LIVING it!

Daughter Melissa, her husband, Todd, and their children, Max and Maddie, arrived from New York on Wednesday. I met them at the airport and felt their arms around me and heard their squeals of delight at returning to the house where they'd spent so many happy hours.

Our middle child, Andy, and his spouse,

Michelle, drove in from Tulsa with Graham and Riley, and we high-fived and wrestled and marveled at Riley's growing vocabulary and Graham's encroaching maturity.

My youngest son, Richard, and his wife, Jennifer, and their daughters, McKenzie and Lexi, came from down the street to mingle with their cousins and in-laws. Andy brought a video he'd produced from old family tapes and pictures that featured Janie's voice and image, and while we cried as we watched it, I think we all felt a sense of deep gratitude to his loving creativity that would allow us always to view her in her prime and to hear her voice at will.

We planned a pilgrimage to her resting place to lay a wreath and to explain to the grandchildren that their "Nini" was only there in body and that her soul was in heaven. That evening, I sat in the chair in front of the fireplace and watched and listened as our family got reacquainted with each other. I heard their stories of "Mom" and their shared memories of her ways, of the happiness she had sprinkled on all of us. They were happy stories, remembrances of the days before she struggled with illness, and I was suddenly aware that the room was filled with happiness—not tears, mind you, but laughter—and it seemed to mingle with an echo of laughter from all those other years when she was with us.

I heard it all. All the 40 years of Christmases past seemed to be in the room with us. I heard Janie's voice again. I saw her smile in the faces of her three children and her grandchildren. I heard her chuckle. I was enveloped in an overwhelming sense of warmth and peace. She was there. Her spirit visited us and saw our efforts to re-create her Christmas, and she approved. She was happy. She was with us. She was ETERNALLY with us!

I felt my cheek, and it was wet. . .

I got up and headed for the front porch before the others noticed.

I looked up into the night sky, wiped away the tears that Janie would have teased me about, and silently offered my thanks to the one whose birth we were celebrating. I thanked him for her peace and for mine, which had come to me only that very evening.

And I knew I would never dread Christmas again.

Angels Can Turn Up in Some of the Unlikeliest Places

Lexi

February 15, 2001 : In a little strip mall on the corner of Oliver and Central dwells an unlikely angel. I know she's an angel because she performs miracles there every day.

She teaches little children to speak.

Her name is Judy Pollard-Licklider.

Judy, a speech therapist, is an unlikely angel because she possesses none of the traits we usually associate with angels save one: love.

She certainly isn't patient when dealing with a bureaucracy—insurance company, state, or otherwise. She will tell you, at the drop of a hat, about how restrictions in health insurance policies, state-funded programs and traditional community grants often impede her work, and how, if she followed their rules, it would condemn her little patients to little or no improvement in their communication skills.

In un-angel-like fashion, she has no tolerance for the forces of impersonalization that reduce her children to case numbers on a report. Her eyes flash as she rages at her own colleagues for accepting mediocrity in their profession. She has been known to salt the language with words that would make an ordinary angel blush when describing the academic debate over the "association" method she uses versus the current method favored by her profession.

As a result of her outspokenness and unwillingness to compromise, Judy is, for the most part, an unfunded as well as unlikely angel. Her Pollard-Licklider Clinic subsists with only the proceeds from grateful parents, some insurance payments and a tiny endowment from her own organization, the Erin is Hope Foundation.

Erin was a patient of Barbara Hull, one of Judy's mentors. She was a little hearing-impaired girl who learned to speak through Hull's application of the "association" method. Erin departed this earth as a young adult, but she was a young adult with a voice, thanks to that method.

Some of Judy's natural combativeness comes from the struggle she had with the public education system in obtaining appropriate schooling for her autistic daughter, Lindsay. Thanks to Judy's intense association method, Lindsay now speaks as if she'd never had a problem. This unlikely angel does love her work, and she loves her patients.

My little granddaughter, Lexi, introduced me to Judy. I stood outside the room with her mother, my daughter-in-law Jennifer, and watched as Judy's one-on-one, in-your-face intervention produced tears in Lexi's eyes and, as a result, mine and Jennifer's.

Lexi was only 17 months old, and Jennifer, with that sense that only a mother has, had known something wasn't quite right. She was first told that Lexi was a late bloomer and that she would eventually speak. Still, plagued by a nagging doubt, Jennifer had Lexi evaluated by two different local agencies. One implied that Lexi was hearing impaired; the other suggested that she be taught sign language so she could communicate. No one, it seemed, knew exactly what was wrong.

No one, that is, until Judy.

"She has a condition called verbal apraxia, and I can have her talking in a year," Jennifer remembers Judy saying. Not "maybe I can help her," but a definite, positive "I can have her talking." Enter hope.

Verbal apraxia, it turns out, is a condition in which the brain fails to learn words. It has nothing to do with the patient's intelligence or cognitive abilities and is often misdiagnosed as retardation or deafness.

In Lexi's case, five minutes with her would convince you that she had neither of those conditions. She would respond to instructions and could make you aware of what she wanted with gestures and little sounds and with a stare that was intense in its determination and heartbreaking in its obvious frustration at speechlessness.

Lexi could understand the world perfectly. She just couldn't make the world understand her. Perhaps because of her condition, she quickly became an iron-willed little girl who could chill you with a look or captivate you with a smile that she flashed when she wanted attention.

It was this tough little cookie that the angel Judy encountered as we stood outside the room and watched through our tears. One determined to teach, the other determined to resist.

Over the next few weeks, Judy's fierce intensity began to take hold. You could see Lexi's eyes shine when she knew she was going to see "Miss Judy" and watch her growing pride at being able to look at a picture of an apple and say "ah-pa-el" or take you through her notebook and point out the vowels that Judy had willed her to learn through countless hours of sheer determination.

You could see the relief in Jennifer's eyes as hopelessness became hope and hope became confidence that her daughter would indeed have speech.

Now, at age 5, Lexi chatters like a little magpie. With the exception of an occasional fractured R, her speech is perfect for a child her age. She's drop-dead gorgeous, confident, ever so saucy and absolutely captivating.

For after all, she was touched by an unlikely angel.

The angel Judy.

Joe Frank Ferguson's Passing Leaves
a Great Big Hole in Country Music

MARCH 15, 2001 : In a hospital room in Fort Worth, Texas, a bit of history passed into eternity last month. Joe Frank Ferguson, one of two surviving members of Bob Wills' pre-wartime Texas Playboys band, was called to his maker.

He was 87.

To understand why his passing was significant, you have to understand how important Bob Wills and the Texas Playboys were to Kansas and Oklahoma during the post-Depression era.

Wills played a brand of music known as Western swing at dances all over within a 400-mile radius of Tulsa. His noontime radio broadcasts over radio station KVOO in Tulsa were heard in the towns and farm communities throughout the station's 50,000-watt coverage area.

In a time when folks didn't have a lot to be happy about, Wills' music made them smile and let them forget their troubles for a while. For $1.25, they could dance the night away to tunes like "San Antonio Rose" or "Faded Love" and hear the latest swing tunes played with a Western flavor that made the music palatable to rural folks.

Wills, you might say, was the Glenn Miller of the West, for his music was a cross between country and the big-band sound so popular during the 1930s.

Steel guitarist Leon McAuliffe, lead guitarist Eldon Shamblin, fiddler Jesse Ashlock, drummer Smokey Dacus, vocalist Tommy Duncan, Joe Frank and countless other band members were all stars in their own right, and their presence on the bandstand was magic to thousands of fans around here.

With Joe Frank's passing, of the original Playboys, only Smokey Dacus survives, and he lies ill and feeble in a rest home in Rogers, Arkansas.

Joe Frank wasn't the first bass player to perform with the Playboys, but he joined at a time when the band was becoming the swing organization that Wills wanted. Wills had just moved to Tulsa and wanted a vocalist who could sing the pop hits of the big-band years, and Joe Frank filled the bill. His high, lilting tenor voice belted out tunes like Irving Berlin's "Marie" and "You're OK" and other standards of the day. He learned to play a standup bass, because Wills told him he couldn't afford to hire another vocalist. The popular Tommy Duncan was already doing vocals.

Joe Frank stayed with the group until the rigors of the road got to him, and he left the band to play closer to home and to raise his family.

I first met him in the '70s, when McAuliffe formed the "Original Texas Playboys" and began touring with the then-surviving members of the band, after Wills died of a stroke in Dallas.

When KFDI began the KFDI/ Charlie Daniels Golf Tournament for Starkey Developmental Center, Leon, Smokey and Joe Frank were the first to volunteer to come to Wichita and perform as celebrities for the tournament. I'll never forget a star-struck Vince Gill, playing guitar in a tournament jam session at Rolling Hills Country Club, saying that he had fulfilled a lifelong dream being on the same bandstand with Leon, Smokey and Joe Frank.

After Leon died in 1985, Smokey would drive from Rogers, Ark., to Oklahoma to pick up Joe Frank, and the two would drive to Wichita to give what they could to Starkey. When Smokey became too ill to come, Joe Frank talked his daughter into driving him up.

Three years ago, after an extended illness, he called me and said the doctor had told him that he could no longer stand the strain of 18 holes of golf, and he said he sure didn't want to "be in the way." We told him that he was wanted and set up a shade on the 18th hole, with three very pretty girls. We called it "Joe Frank's hole," and the idea was that he would putt for each team that came up on the hole. Then the team could use his putt if it was better than theirs, which it frequently was.

"Joe Frank's hole" became the hit of the tournament for the next three years, and his still perfect-pitch voice was always a highlight of our Stars for Starkey Concert. I noticed last year that while he was on stage singing "Marie," all of the artists backstage had stopped their visiting and were watching Joe Frank wow 'em one more time.

The last time I saw him was in Fort Worth at Red Steagall's Cowboy Gathering. He got up and sang with the Western swing band while more than 1,000 dancers stood and applauded. After his performance, I went over and congratulated him. He stood up, hugged me and said, "If the good Lord's willin' I'll see you in Wichita at the tournament, in June."

Well, the good Lord wasn't willing. I figure that maybe he's a Western swing fan, and he needed a little guy with a big heart and perfect pitch who could play a little bass and make folks smile, so he called Joe Frank up to sing.

It was His gain, and our loss.

What's a Vacation Without a Little Adventure?

MARCH 29, 2001 : There I am, talking into a TV camera, describing how the brave California Highway Patrol officers captured the bad guys and retrieved my stolen car. Overhead there's a police helicopter buzzing around. Around me are at least a dozen patrol cars, officers running around with bulletproof vests on and three scowling car thieves, handcuffed and staring at me like I ate their Happy Meal before they could sit down! Vic Scholfield is describing the chase to his wife on the cell phone, and both of us feel like Starsky and Hutch.

But to explain how Vic the car dealer and Ol' Mike the retired disc jockey came to be in the middle of this crime wave, I should digress.

See, at Vic's invitation, I drove my motor home out to Indio, California last month to see what all the fuss was about. A bunch of Wichitans migrate to the desert each winter and stay till the end of March, soaking up the sun and playing golf, while the rest of us freeze our extremities off in the typical Kansas winter.

Traveling in a motor home actually makes the trip affordable, so I loaded the old girl up and headed out. After two and a half days of serious driving, and surviving the mother of all blizzards in Flagstaff, Arizona, I wound up in the tropical 75-degree climate that, once experienced, explained the annual migration.

Vic had spread the word that a new golf pigeon was in the area, and at least 15 transplanted golf hustlers were waiting for me in eager anticipation of picking my pocket on some of the 110 area golf courses.

The pattern was set from the first day. Wake up. Take my dog Ranger for his walk. Go to a golf course. Pay Vic and his buddies. Eat lunch. Play golf again. Pay Vic and his buddies. Take Ranger for a walk. Go to dinner. Take Ranger for a walk again. Go to bed.

Soon, I knew not what day it was or even what course we were playing. When you're a golf pigeon, time has a way of slowing to a crawl.

After several days, a break in the routine came when the clouds opened up and, uncharacteristically, it rained in the desert for three solid days. Vic suggested that I wire home for more money during the down time, which of course I did.

Now, mind you, I was staying in a gated motor home park with an 8-foot wall around it for security purposes. Each night I parked my car in front of the motor home and parked a little red scooter (for scooting around in the park) on the patio.

On the first rainy day, I hid from the same golf hustlers who figured they could turn me into a gin rummy pigeon also. On the second rainy day, I got up, took Ranger out and immediately noticed that my little red scooter was GONE!

"Those nice motor home neighbors must have put it back in the coach bay because it was raining," I said to myself as I took Ranger to the pet area. When I returned, I looked in the bay of the coach - NO SCOOTER!

Then it dawned on me — NO CAR!

As panic set in, I looked up and saw a police car slowly coming down the street, pursued by 10 or 12 angry motor home folks who were missing cars, bicycles, cell phones and car radios. Amid the screaming and shouting, I filed a stolen car (and scooter) report. Then I remembered: I have On Star! Yes, my tow car was equipped with what I figured was a useless gadget, and I remembered the salesman saying, "If it's ever stolen. . . ."

I called On Star; they immediately reported that the car was parked at 62nd Avenue and Jackson Street in Thermal, a neighboring community. The officer dispatched the Highway Patrol, and Vic and I jumped into Vic's car (he'd dropped by to see if I wanted to play marbles for money) and away we went to 62nd and Jackson.

Because it was raining, the desert roads were muddy, and the Highway Patrol officer we encountered was waiting for a four-wheel drive vehicle to go to the area where On Star had last reported the car. The four-wheel-drive arrived; the two officers took off down a muddy road after warning Starsky - er, Vic and me to stay behind.

In a moment they came tearing out of the desert and headed to a residential area where the aforementioned helicopter and On Star had spotted the car, now moving. Vic and I followed at a safe distance. When the occupants of the car realized they had been spotted, they bailed out of my car with the stuff they'd stripped out of it, and into their car, and a high-speed chase began (with Vic and me bringing up the rear).

It was over in minutes. After driving into a front yard and scattering, the culprits were chased down on foot in the neighborhood, handcuffed and placed in the patrol cars. My car was returned in reasonably good shape, considering it had been stripped of radio, CD player and speakers, and the ringleader, a three-time parolee, was looking at jail time. As of this writing, the little red scooter has not been recovered, and Vic and I have not received, as we'd hoped we might, any offers for a cops series on TV.

I did come home and pay my On Star bill, though!

Thinking of Buying an RV? Ol' Mike Can Help You

APRIL 5, 2001 : In an effort to do something constructive with the space allotted to me by this newspaper, I now present the first of two public service columns designed to aid and enlighten you, dear reader, on matters wherein I have particular experience or knowledge.

Our subject today is: recreational vehicles.

Oh, don't deny it! I KNOW you've secretly wondered what it would be like to go careering down the highway in a motor home as big as Goddard, with a big goofy grin plastered on your countenance, as cars, trucks, buses and pedestrians scramble to get out of your path.

I know you've secretly coveted the freedom of taking off, bound for parts unknown, ready after a lifetime of toil to explore America's highways and byways.

I know you've dreamt of tooting those big air horns just as somebody's blue-haired aunt was walking her Chihuahua across the intersection in front of you.

Yes, and I know your doubts and fears also. Can you actually drive one? Can you afford one? How much fuel do they consume? How do you deal with all that, uh, waste material that collects? Where do you park one so that it won't trigger a petition to get you forcibly removed from the neighborhood?

Yes, I understand. For, you see, I once dreamed those dreams and dreaded those doubts and fears, until I became the proud owner of my first RV. I (along with the bank) have owned four RVs since my Janie dragged me, kicking and screaming, into the RV factory where we bought our first.

Suffice it to say that the lifestyle surpasses even our early expectations and indeed has become a rewarding and fulfilling pastime that has nurtured me through the difficult retirement jitters that I faced early on.

Hence, I now feel compelled to help you, dear reader, in your decision -making process to acquire or not to acquire.

You need several things to become an RV person.

First, of course, you will need an RV. RVs come in all sizes and shapes, price ranges and commitments—from Uncle Charlie's converted 74 Volkswagen van to tent campers to 45-foot luxury buses like the ones country music stars and campaigning politicians ride around in. It doesn't matter what you start out with; you will likely trade it within a year, as no self-respecting RV owner owns the same one for very long. He ALWAYS covets the next bigger one!

Other things you'll need:

A little yappy dog on a chain. This is mandatory. All RV people must have a nasty, cranky little dog that will bare his teeth at other RV people's dogs while on his way to the pet area in any campground.

A brown polyester jumpsuit is also required. Red is acceptable, but brown is preferred. (I don't know why.)

A wooden sign that says, "We're spending our kids' inheritance" to nail on the back end of your RV.

Some little plastic rooster, chicken, bunny

rabbit and duck lights to string up around the RV when you're in the park. (In lieu of these lights, you can substitute some plastic pink flamingos, but they're sort of hard to find.)

A ball cap for the man that says "old goat" across the front. A T-shirt that says the same thing can be substituted.

A map of the United States that shows a sticker for every state in which you've camped. Flags from the states can be substituted, provided they're arranged across the front of the RV where they can't be missed.

A really good sewer hose that doesn't leak is a flat-out must. It's also helpful to have something that will keep the hose from gyrating out of the sewer when dumping is taking place.

A ball cap for the woman that says "old goat's wife."

A good pair of walking shoes, for walking around the campground in the morning, staring at other people's vehicles.

A Camping World membership (the RV person's Disneyland).

A really BIG toolbox with all kinds of tools, including duct tape and Velcro, for use when you break down. The more tools, the more confused you'll be, and the more likely to call a road service as opposed to trying to fix it yourself.

A really good marriage, for those times when your wife, the navigator, told you to turn left when you should have turned right, or when you backed over the picnic table while she was directing you into your parking space.

Cancer That Was Once Beaten Rears Its Ugly Head Again

APRIL 19, 2001 : I have something rather personal to tell you. I have bladder cancer. That's right. The big C, which I thought was whipped two years ago, has come back to bedevil my retirement and cause me the miseries. See, two and a half years ago, I was diagnosed with this stuff.

That was the bad news.

The good news was that I had the kind that could be effectively treated by removing from my blankety-blank bladder the five surface tumors my doctor found. That was followed with a form of chemotherapy that would trigger the body's immune system and defeat the other tumors that were likely to reappear, as they are prone to do in the kind of cancer I had.

The surgery inside my bladder was performed (never mind how they got in there), the chemo was administered, and after a while, three more tumors appeared and were exorcised the same way, with the same follow-up treatment. Subsequent examinations revealed no return of the tumors until a few weeks ago, when one "low grade" tumor reared its little head.

During the surgery to get rid of this latest invasion of my poor mistreated bladder, the doctor discovered that the cancer might now be penetrating the bladder lining, which would ultimately lead to it getting out of the bladder and invading other parts of the body. The most commonly prescribed treatment for that predicament is complete removal of the bladder before the cancer begins its journey through the bladder walls. Once the bladder is removed, the surgeon can sometimes fashion a replacement out of small intestine and hook you back up to your regular plumbing, and you basically function the same as always. Sometimes the only solution is a small bag worn outside that collects the waste from the kidneys and is emptied at regular intervals. A variation of that is an illeal conduit, in which a reservoir is fashioned that collects the waste and is emptied by a catheter. While some other forms of chemotherapy are being tested, these treatments are the prescribed methods for being sure that the cancer doesn't clobber you.

As you can probably tell, I'm not real thrilled about any of the prospects that await me. I am, however, thrilled that there is treatment that is life sparing and that is available. I've talked to many men who've been down the same path and have learned that once done, none of the above outcomes interferes with a full, healthy lifestyle, and once gotten used to, they are no big deal.

I'm interviewing doctors at Johns Hopkins Medical Center in Baltimore and at Memorial Sloan-Kettering Cancer Center in New York to decide how I'll be treated. I've been to the Mayo Clinic in Rochester, Minnesota to confirm the diagnosis and will probably schedule the treatment in the next few weeks.

I've learned in life that there is nothing more boring than listening to somebody's ailments, and the main reason I'm covering mine is to focus some awareness on this kind of cancer.

There are approximately 50,000 new cases of bladder cancer every year in the United States; it is the fourth most common form of cancer in men (prostate is first). Caught early, bladder cancer almost never results in death, and many times it can be arrested and held at bay with the chemotherapy I described above.

Symptoms include (1) blood in your urine, (2) frequent urination and (3) painful urination. Those symptoms, by the way, are not always indications of cancer, but your doctor should be consulted IMMEDIATELY if you detect them.

I have to tell you that I'm scared as hell!

I don't like hospitals, and I don't like doctors whacking around on my person, nor do I look forward to losing any body parts. I've learned a new respect for the multitudes of friends I've had who've already bravely faced this stuff, and I hope I can deal with it as many of them have.

In other words, I'm going to try not to whine and to count the blessings that I have in the positive prognosis that I think I still have. I will, with your permission, keep you posted on my progress from time to time.

I'll say one thing, getting old ain't for sissies!

A Little Time with the Grandkids Renews a Weary Soul

APRIL 26, 2001 : I have a friend who often comments that the great thing about grandchildren is that "you can play with them, then put them up."

My problem is, I don't want to "put them up." I want to take them home with me.

I'm in New York City as I write this, reeling from the bladder cancer diagnosis that I told you about last week. I came first to Johns Hopkins in Baltimore, then on to New York for a long-planned Easter visit with my daughter and son-in-law, Melissa and Todd McDermott, and their two children, Max and Maddie. While I'm here, I'll be visiting Sloan-Kettering Hospital for yet another perspective on the treatment I'll need.

I'll admit I came rather depressed and self-absorbed in the old "why me?" syndrome. The last thing I expected was to be uplifted and encouraged by two little people whose sweetness and enthusiasm swept away the depression that a serious illness had sprinkled upon me.

From the moment I entered Melissa and Todd's Lower East Side apartment, I was in my grandkids' care, no longer allowed to dwell on the unpleasantness of adult worries. It was Maddie's ninth birthday, and besides, Easter was on its way and they were out of school, and their Grandpaw was here and there were a million things to be done.

I was peppered with questions, pummeled with hugs and kisses, tugged this way and that, engaged in all matter of conversation. "Could we play blackjack? Are we going to the movies? Can we go to the toy store? How long are you going to stay? How about us going to the comic book store?"

In no time flat, I was a kid just like them, and my troubles didn't seem to matter much anymore. All that mattered was their smiles, or the feel of a little hand in mine leading me to yet another wonder of the big-city life that had stolen them from me all too soon.

"Will they take your bladder out?" the now 9-year-old Maddie asked, curled up in my lap just before bedtime. "Probably," I answered. "Will it hurt?" Max asked. "Maybe a little," I said. "Not if you close your eyes and sing 'Twinkle Twinkle Little Star' while they're giving you a shot," Maddie said. "That's what I do when I go to the doctor, and it doesn't hurt!" Max, who is 10 going on 36, chimed in, "Mike, don't worry. You'll get well, and I think you should sing the ABCs because it keeps you from crying and it's more manly."

That was all the time these two allowed me to devote to my pity party. They were on to bigger and better things.

I think when God invented grandchildren and passed them on to us, he was giving us the most thoughtful gift of all. Grandchildren give us a chance to associate with innocence at a time in our lives when innocence seems forever lost. Grandkids give us a chance to get it right the second time around. We have the same opportunity when we're raising our own kids, but the pressure of making a living sometimes clouds our ability to savor the sweetness of childhood.

Then, too, there's the fact that none of us are really experienced in the art of listening to children. By the time we figure it out, our own children, busy with their lives, aren't really interested in talking to us anymore.

But grandkids are interested in everything you have to say. They have a million questions to ask and a million more observations to share, and since their moms and dads are busy (like we were), they need a big person to pat and cuddle and take them to the toy store on their time schedule instead of the world's.

The neat thing about this whole plan is that, provided we can break old habits, we now have the time. This window comes along, for most of us, when life has slowed us down a bit and gives us pause for reflection. I can think of no finer use of that reflection time than to wrap up in the warmth and adoration of grandchildren.

I did pretty darn well in the grandchild department. I have six, and all possess their own sparkle and personality. Graham is dependable and creative; Riley is happy and merry; Mackenzie is sweet and dependable; Lexi is both charming and independent; Max is thoughtful and studious; Maddie is bright and industrious. They all radiate the sweetness and goodness that is their grandmother's legacy, and though I miss her terribly, I see her in each of our grandchildren.

If Easter is a time for renewal, then mine was successful. The doctors gave me the information I needed to decide on treatment. I find I need not worry about my daughter and son-in-law, as they seem well entrenched in their big-city careers, and Max and Maddie successfully reminded their grandfather that life is well worth the struggle, no matter what bumps in the road may appear.

My grandkids cried a little when I left, and I assured them that we'd see each other again in a few weeks, hugged Melissa, shook Todd's hand, and crawled into the cab for the airport.

I'm sure, though, that the cabbie wondered why the old guy in the back seat had wet eyes and was singing the ABCs under his breath.

Things Would Be Different If I Had a Second Chance

May 3, 2001 : When an illness comes to visit, you sort of get, you know, philosophical. So I've been thinking lately about the things I'd do differently if I had another go-around at life.

Oh, I'd make some changes, all right! Not that I've been that unhappy with the way my life has turned out, but I can definitely list some improvements I'd make were I to get an instant replay.

Don't get me wrong. I'm not planning on going to that big radio station in the sky anytime soon, but shoot, I could REALLY improve things if I could just kinda rewind and apply what I know now to what I THOUGHT I knew back then.

I'd work less and play more.

I grew up thinking it was a sin to slack at a job, and I believed up until I retired that work came above all else if you wanted to properly support your family. Now safely anchored on the other side of earning a living, I find I can't remember much at all about the work that kept me away from home most of the day and the weekends, but I CAN remember the pleas of tiny children's voices to "Play with me" and "Take me fishing." And I can clearly hear my Janie's sweet voice pleading with me to come home at a decent hour.

I hear it every day of my life now.

I'd cultivate friends better.

I was so work-absorbed that I didn't have many friends that weren't employees or customers, and truthfully, they were great acquaintances, but I rarely took the time to be a real friend to them and had little to discuss with them outside of the business. Now, looking back, I'd be more involved in their lives and the things that interested them. Janie kept up with those details, and I leaned on her for the little niceties that foster friendships. You can't imagine the void that exists in that area now that her memories are no longer accessible to me.

I'd pet my dog more.

Dogs love you unconditionally, and it's worthwhile, I think, to return that love to them. Since dogs don't ask for much more than contact with their master, I'd make sure that my dog always felt as loved as he made me feel. My old dog, Traveler, died in '91, and I wonder every day if I petted him enough those 15 years that he shadowed me.

I'd call people on their birthdays.

I tended to forget birthdays, not realizing, I guess, how profound it is to receive a phone call on your birthday. Now that I reflect, someone was always nice enough to remember mine, and it made me feel important and special. If I could, I'd go back and return the favor to all those folks who were so thoughtful to me.

I would spend more time with my grandmother.

She knew our family history, and she lived through the turn of the previous century, and I can see now that she longed to share that history with her grandchildren. I was usually too busy or too much in a hurry to really listen. Now, given the chance, I'd sit at her feet and dwell on her every word so she'd know that her life was interesting and important to those she loved. When she passed away, much of our family history died with her. I wouldn't let that happen again.

I'd listen to my mom play the piano.

Mom played both piano and violin, and she played beautifully. Some of my earliest memories are of her practicing Beethoven and Bach while I sat on the front porch of our Marfa, Texas, home, dreaming in the afternoon sun. The music she made was the soundtrack for those days when I didn't have a care or a worry and life was uncomplicated. She didn't play so much in her later years, but if I could live it all again I'd pester her every day to play for me. I'd try to memorize every note, so I could close my eyes at any time and journey back to those afternoons on the front porch when everything was right with the world.

I'd discipline my kids less and talk to them more.

I was pretty stern and tough when they were growing up, and I equated firmness with love. Now I'd take a lesson from their mother and be softer and more understanding of their little transgressions, and I'd try explaining things more and demanding things less. They'd tell you today that they understand why I was like I was, but it would sure be nice if I could retool my image with them and be remembered as less of a meany and more of a softy. I think I'd like myself better if that were the case.

Well, unfortunately, God doesn't hand out second chances. He makes us live with what we have been. But he DOES grant us the grace to reflect on the past with an eye toward the future, and the ability to use those life lessons to reshape the future to a more pleasing performance.

Sometimes, as in my case, he gives us a little nudge to kick start the process.

Readers Give Ol' Mike a Humbling
Lesson in Kindness Shared

May 17, 2001 : If you have been the recipient of kindness from another human being, you know how profoundly significant it can be. It engulfs you with a warm, comforting glow that inspires confidence, reassurance and appreciation.

I write these words now, having been the fortunate recipient of such kindness in thought and deed since my column on my bladder cancer situation. I've received hundreds of e-mails, phone calls and well-wishes from people I know and many more from people I haven't met yet.

The overwhelming outpouring of kindness has helped me deal with what I'd have to describe as a bummer of a diagnosis and come to grips with the fact that in spite of an unsettling fate, I'm indeed a very lucky person. Lucky because my cancer is treatable and should not be life-threatening, and lucky because so many people have reminded me that folks are, in fact, caring, concerned and, yes, kind.

People with far more problems have reached out to assure me that I'll be all right. People with stories of unbelievable hardship have shared them with me; people with miraculous outcomes to impossible situations have graciously discussed their cases with me in the hopes that they would cheer me.

And they have.

Next Monday, I'll be at Johns Hopkins in Baltimore, and the surgery that I've dreaded and worried about will be performed. I'll be in the hospital for seven to 10 days, barring unforeseen complications. I'll probably be fortified with all manner of drugs, but more importantly, I'll be fortified with the blanket of kindness that has covered me since I first wrote about my illness.

I deem that wave of kindness to be a saving grace that will get me through what I'm told will be a few very uncomfortable days.

Anyway, after reflecting these last few days on how fortunate I am, I gathered some thoughts about kindness that I offer up for your consideration:

Kindness sweetens the character in a way no other trait does. The giver of kindness is instantly rewarded with a sense of accomplishment and personal satisfaction. The kind people whom I know have no self-image problems. They are happy with themselves and radiate that happiness in their countenance.

Kindness is replicated in ways that many times are unknown to the originator. If someone has been kind to you, you will be inspired to be kind to someone else, and before you know it you will have launched your own act of kindness into a world that is sadly deficient of overall compassion, and you will have truly made a difference.

Kindness promotes kindness. The law of reciprocity demands that if you are kind to someone, they in turn will not be able to rest until they have returned the kindness. If you feel a void of kindness, try offering some to those who've been stingy, and watch what happens.

Kindness defines your feelings about a person. Think about the people you care about the most. I'd be willing to bet that they are kind to you above all else.

Kindness bolsters the recipient. If you want to uplift a person who is sad or depressed or fearful, nothing does the job like a simple act of kindness. Try it, and watch the sunshine creep into his or her smile.

Kindness disarms your enemies. Find an opportunity to be kind to someone with whom you don't get along, and observe the transformation. It's impossible to hate someone who is sincerely kind to you.

I have observed over the years that, for the most part, everyone is capable of kindness. However, it would be Pollyannaish to suggest that everyone is kind. Some folks are just plain mean. Some folks are that way because no one ever took the time to show them kindness. It is they who need your kindness the most.

I saw a bumper sticker the other day that said something like, "I'm committing random acts of kindness and senseless acts of love," and thought to myself that it would make a great sermon for some preacher.

As for me, I'll journey to Baltimore armed with the kindness you have showered upon me and secure in the knowledge that I am indeed most fortunate to be so considered.

You have been way too kind.

With Cancer Surgery Over, Each Day Is Full of Thanks

JUNE 14, 2001 : I felt like I was drowning. That's the only way I can describe the sensation. Drowning in a tube or pipe that was so tight that I couldn't raise my arms. It seemed like water was swooshing all around and rushing me to the top of this tube, and I was gagging for breath with no way to communicate it to anyone who cared. I tried, but my voice just sounded like a roar coming out of a parchment-dry throat.

Then, almost magically, I could breathe. I saw my daughter Melissa's sweet face and heard her voice off in the distance in an eerie echo. "Dad . . . Dad . . . Are you awake? Can you hear me? Are you OK?"

"Water" was all I could say. Then I heard a nurse saying that I couldn't have any water just yet. Instead, she gave me a small, damp sponge and told me to rinse my mouth with it. (I can still taste that sponge!) The next sensation was immense pain in my middle section. I complained to no one in particular, and remember a nurse saying, "Sir, you've just had major surgery; there will be some pain."

I hadn't been drowning. I was coming out of the surgery, and the water sensation had been the ICU team removing tubing from my nose and mouth as they wheeled me to the Intensive Care Unit of Johns Hopkins Hospital. The pain (which I wasn't supposed to feel) was coming from a misplaced epidermal IV in my back. After they got around to adjusting it, the pain disappeared.

I'd come to Johns Hopkins three days earlier to make ready for the surgery that would remove my cancerous bladder, my prostate and a piece of my small intestine which would be fashioned into a "neo-bladder" so that I could still function normally. I'd had one last meal in Baltimore's Little Italy on Friday, then locked myself in a hotel room Saturday and Sunday in preparation for the operation.

The prep is simple: Drink something that tastes like turpentine, stay close to the bathroom, eat nothing and hope you don't die before you wake.

After 24 hours in the intensive care unit, they rolled me to the floor where I'd spend the next 11 days being poked, prodded, stuck, bled, measured and systematically robbed of all dignity. I was not allowed any solid food for eight days. They had me confused with a Hindu on a hunger strike.

I began walking that Tuesday, and graduated from a few steps the first day to walking the entire hallway within a couple of days. This was no small feat. I was tethered to a little blue machine that beeped every time I made a wrong move or ran out of the 21 different medicines they were pumping into me. (OK, it was three different kinds.) In addition, certain lower extremities were swollen beyond recognition, which made my walk more of a waddle. Days ran together into a blur, and my strength increased gradually. I had all kinds of tubes sticking out of me and all kinds of IVs sticking in me, but somehow things began to get better. I began to think that I might actually get to come home on Tuesday, eight days after the operation.

The doctor, however, said "not yet" after

checking me over. We set a new goal of exiting that coming Friday. On Thursday, though, I got a fever, caused by an infected IV line, which precluded a Friday exit. Good antibiotics cleared that up, and I was released Saturday morning.

In the air on the way home, I had a chance to reflect on my fate. I'd come from being scared out of my wits with the diagnosis of cancer to a near-perfect resolution of the problem by the surgery I'd undergone. My body was now free of the disease. The operation had gone exactly as I'd wanted it, too. The surgery was the easiest part, the prep, anticipation and aftermath being the toughest.

I'd received over 250 "get well" cards from people all over Kansas. I was on hundreds of prayer lists; my room was full of flowers that had cheered me each day as another bunch arrived.

I could now write the final chapter to "Ol' Mike's bladder saga" with the knowledge that I am, indeed, most fortunate. Where once only a shadow hovered over me, I now walk in the bright sunlight and wake up each day thankful for modern medicine and for the angels that I call my friends and for all those prayers that were offered up for me.

They worked!

Family Pool Is Where Memories Are Enshrined

JUNE 21, 2001 : I think I'm getting more sentimental with each passing year. I find myself getting more and more attached to things. Inanimate objects, objects that don't breathe or speak. Lifeless objects, like my swimming pool.

We built that pool nearly 30 years ago. I remember how we agonized over whether we could afford it. After all, it would cost almost $8,000! We concluded, though, after saving for two years, that it would indeed be a good investment for the kids and the family, and contracted with the Mattingly Co. to build it.

I'll never forget getting a panicky call at work from Janie: "They've dug up the entire back yard! It's so BIG!" As it turned out, it literally engulfed the back yard and dominated the area.

The pool, as we'd hoped, quickly became the center of family activity between May and September. Our cookouts with friends, birthday parties, slumber parties all revolved around that pool.

Janie and I often found ourselves just holding onto a float and talking as we floated effortlessly in its placid water, discussing the trials and tribulations of our days. It was a special, quiet time that we reserved for ourselves two or three evenings a week. Clinging to that float, we schemed and planned and dreamed about what was to be as we raised those three precious kids and built a life together.

It wasn't all peaches and cream. A pool is a lot of upkeep. We live in an area with an abundance of trees, which translates into stuff falling into the pool, which in turn translates into a lot of vacuuming and cleaning. Then there are the chemicals, the equipment, pumps and heaters that periodically break down.

You have to "close" the pool each year and "open" it each spring. As the kids grew, cleaning the pool became a way to earn their allowance, and while it wasn't their favorite chore, they all became adept at it.

As the years passed and the children drifted off to college and lives of their own, we used the pool less and less. It fell to our "home manager" Janie and a local pool service to maintain it. My responsibilities at work kept me away more and more, and I swam less and less. Jane's grandmother duties kicked in with the arrival of our first grandchildren, and her pool activity consisted of sitting on the side and supervising a new crop of beginning swimmers. And for a while the pool had a resurgence.

"I think we should consider covering it up," Janie said to me one day. She pointed out that we hardly ever used it; the grandkids were scattered around the country, and we were spending more time cleaning it than using it. That was the last time we spoke of it. Her illness made its ugly presence known that winter, the pool was closed, and it became the least of our worries.

I was sitting out on the patio enjoying a morning cup of tea the other day, listening to the morning and reveling in the quiet, when I thought of that conversation we'd had about covering up the pool. I turned to survey the blue water that was actually sparkling in the morning sun, and I swear I heard laughter.

For ever so brief a moment, I saw my children when they were still small enough for me to toss into the air when we played sea monster.

I heard the shrieks of delight as I chased them around the pool.

I saw a brave little Andy pleading for all present to "watch me" as he mustered the courage to jump off the board for the first time.

I saw Melissa learning to lean forward enough to actually dive in.

I heard Richard giggling as he cannonballed Jane in her favorite lawn chair.

I saw Jane chuckling and holding court on the side as the kids vied for her attention.

I saw the two of us floating and planning in the cool of the evening.

The laughter and squeals of two generations of kids echoed through the morning haze and overwhelmed me. I was engulfed with 30 years of memories, all centered around that pool. That morning it dawned on me that the pool isn't an inanimate object or a thing.

It's a pool of memories. Pleasant memories. Memories that are indelibly etched on my heart.

No, sir, I don't reckon we'll be covering that old pool up anytime soon.

Not in my lifetime, anyway.

Grudges Aren't Worth the Price We Pay to Carry Them

JULY 5, 2001 : One of the most debilitating human traits is the inability to forgive. Some of us simply can't let go of past slights. We harbor and nurture grudges as if they were some kind of treasure to be hoarded and counted throughout our lives. We love rehearsing the endless details of a disagreement or wrong as if it were a badge of accomplishment rather than what it actually is, a ticket to bitterness that only hardens as the years pass and makes us sour and disagreeable in our old age. Families, friendships and businesses have been torn apart by this strange and disheartening human condition.

It's on my mind as I write, for two reasons.

Since we just celebrated the Fourth of July, I was thinking about two old American revolutionaries, Thomas Jefferson and John Adams. They were great contemporaries during the founding of the nation and were good friends during the upheaval that gave birth to our country.

Some political disagreements, however, separated Adams the Federalist and Jefferson the Populist to the point that they gradually became bitter enemies and for many years refused to have anything to do with each other. Both went on to serve as President of the United States, which they had helped create, and both were immensely distinguished in their service to their country.

In their later years they began exchanging polite letters. Historians tell us that through their correspondence they rediscovered their friendship and found a common ground. Their correspondence tells of how much each looked forward to receiving the other's letters and how their lives were enriched by the renewal of their friendship.

Oddly, both lived to see the Declaration of Independence they had crafted celebrate its 50th anniversary. Jefferson died shortly after midnight July 4, 1826, and Adams died later that day. Adams' last words were, "At least Jefferson still survives," not knowing that his old friend had preceded him in death by just a few hours.

You have to wonder what could have been, had these two giants of men been able to quickly put aside their petty differences and collaborate on the country's formation instead of being enemies all those years. You also have to wonder how much their lives would have been enriched by a lifelong friendship.

The second reason I was thinking about this was that a few weeks ago I got a call out of the blue from the object of one of my grudges.

We'd been band members together in another lifetime in El Paso, when my biggest ambition was to be a country music star. Our little group appeared on local radio and TV, and the Trailblazers, as we were called, was a pretty hot group in our area. We were a democratic organization with no real leader, and gradually disagreements and arguments over who should do what wore us down and we split up.

I went on to form another group that played around town until I left to come to

Wichita in 1964. The other part of the band also regrouped under the leadership of this fellow, and for a time we were competitors and harbored bad feelings about each other that were never resolved.

Nearly 40 years later, he called to say that he'd heard I was facing a challenge and that he would pray for me. He said that he'd followed my career all these years, and that he often thought, as I had, about how much fun we'd had in our little band and how pleasant those memories were.

We discovered that we both had kids who were making us proud and that we both shared a passion for golf, and for the life of us, neither could remember what the issues were that separated us. We vowed to get together on a golf course in the near future and catch up on each other's lives.

As we hung up that day, I reflected again on the foolhardiness of a 40-year grudge. I felt like a weight had been lifted from my shoulders, and I resolved to search my past for any other grudges that might be lurking and to take time to exorcize those also.

Life is just too short to carry 'em around anymore.

OL' MIKE AND THE TRAILBLAZERS

Death Takes a Gentleman and a Genius of Country Music

JULY 12, 2001 : When I was a boy, my grandmother had a little restaurant in Snyder, Texas. I spent two months there one summer washing dishes, busing tables and generally trying to earn my $2.50-a-week allowance.

It was there that I became acquainted with Chet Atkins.

I didn't meet him until many years later, but I became acquainted with him through his records on my grandmother's old Wurlitzer jukebox there in the Hob Nob Cafe on the main drag in Snyder. I figured out a way to play the songs I wanted to hear by pushing a little button on the back, and it kept me from having to put my hard-earned nickels in to hear the music.

Chet had two records on the jukebox that got my attention: "Meet Mr. Callahan" and "Downhill Drag." I played them over and over and secretly wished I could play a guitar like that.

It was about that time that I became interested in the guitar, and when I returned home that summer I lobbied for one, and my folks got me a pawn shop special for Christmas. The guitar became my constant companion and triggered my interest in country music, and I began reading everything I could get my hands on about country stars and the music, and especially about Chet Atkins.

In those days, his career was just starting to take off and he was becoming well known. He'd played with the likes of the Carter family, Homer and Jethro, Bill Carlisle and others, and had finally made his way to Nashville and was appearing regularly on the Grand Ol' Opry, both as a featured soloist and as a backup player. He played a "finger style" electric guitar after the fashion of Merle Travis, one of country music's most famous guitar players, and also coveted the style of Django Reinhardt, a jazz player from the 1920s and '30s.

In 1960, I was selected Mr. DJ USA and flown to Nashville to appear on WSM and the Grand Ol' Opry. It was my first trip to Music City and my first airplane ride. While I was there, I met all my heroes, including Eddy Arnold, Hank Snow, Patsy Cline and more. The biggest thrill, however, was meeting Chet.

One night they took me to a little club in Printers Alley where Chet was performing. I stepped outside to get some fresh air and there he was, taking a break from his performance. We chatted for a few moments, about what I don't remember, but I do remember how kind and friendly he was to this wet-nosed kid from El Paso. By that time, Chet was becoming the head of all of the artists and repertoire at RCA records and was recording artists like Elvis Presley, Jim Reeves, Roger Miller, Perry Como, Waylon Jennings, Don Gibson, Skeeter Davis and, of course, himself. Soon he was being hailed as the driving force behind the Nashville sound that propelled the growth of country music from regional music to a national craze. He was also arguably the most famous guitar player in the world.

My next contact with him, besides playing his records on KFDI regularly, was when we brought him, Boots Randolph and Floyd Cramer to Century II for a sold-out concert in the '70s. One other time during the early '80s I booked him for a pops concert with the Wichita Symphony, much to the consternation of the orchestra manager, who wasn't sure that a hick guitar player could perform in front of real musicians. After I played him Chet's recording with Arthur Fiedler and the Boston Pops Orchestra, he was convinced, and Chet sold out Century II again.

My last contact with him was in 1989, when we again booked him to appear with members of the Wichita Symphony for the Chamber of Commerce's annual meeting. Again, he wowed them with his humor, versatility and marvelous music.

By that time he had basically retired from the recording business, had left RCA and was experimenting with different styles of music, from jazz to fusion rock. He'd become, against his will, a Nashville icon.

He often said that he was sorry he'd taken country music so far to the pop side during his tenure as the head of RCA in Nashville, and that in many ways he believed he'd helped homogenize one of the last truly pure forms of American music, and regretted it. In the last decade of his life, he fought cancer, played golf, turned up on an occasional country music TV special, recorded some, and lived the life of a true "Country Gentleman," the title of one of his best recordings.

If you're not a country music fan, Chet's passing was probably not a significant event in your life. For me, and I suspect a lot of others, it brought tears and represented the end of an era.

We'll not see his like again.

Another Health Concern Intrudes on Everyday Life

AUGUST 2, 2001 : Just when I thought it was safe to pass a doctor's office without stopping! If you read this column regularly, or even sporadically, you know about yours truly's bout with bladder cancer. It culminated in a trip to Johns Hopkins, where the cancerous bladder was removed and a new bladder built.

What I didn't tell you was that just before I came home, I got a fever, which caused the doctors at Hopkins to run a series of tests to determine its origin. Turns out that the cause was an infected IV line. One of the tests they ran, however, a CT scan, revealed a growth in my right chest area that needed a biopsy.

Since I was coming home in two days, I declined any more poking and prodding that would delay my departure. We decided that the biopsy could be done when I came back in August for a checkup.

While recuperating these last two months at home, I began to notice a tightening in my neck and a swelling just over my right collarbone, and I developed a dry cough which, on reflection, began back in March prior to my trip to Hopkins. As these symptoms increased, I turned myself in to my doctor, who immediately ordered a new CT scan that confirmed that there was indeed a mass developing at a rapid rate in my chest and throat area.

Five days later, I was biopsied at Via Christi, and two days after that I was sitting in front of oncologist David Johnson, being told that I have something called "diffuse large cell B lymphoma, stage two (bulky)." Two days after that I was sitting in a chair in the Kansas Cancer Center, receiving the first of six doses of chemotherapy.

In that short period of time, I experienced all the emotions that such a diagnosis brings. First, panic. Then, hope that it's just some simple infection. Then, hope that if it's cancer its Hodgkin's (the easiest to treat), then, resignation that it's not (it's a non-Hodgkin's variety), then, fear of chemotherapy, then fear that it can't be cured. *Will I lose my hair? Will I be sick? Am I a dead man walking?*

That's all the bad news to date.

There is, if you can believe it, some good news.

Fortunately, because the diagnosis and treatment came in such rapid succession, I didn't have much time to spend with those fears. Also, because we caught it early (stage two), there is a 50-to-70 percent cure probability.

Because it's fast-growing, the cure probability is enhanced. (Fast-growing cells are easier to kill.)

The chemo, so far, hasn't made me sick.

I still have my hair.

The nurses are really nice.

The swelling, tightness and cough disappeared within three days after the first treatment.

I still got to go to Colorado.

I lost 37 pounds between the bladder deal and this darn thing.

The white blood cell booster shots don't hurt.

After the chemo, I will need some radiation, but as I mentioned, the prognosis is good.

I have learned a few things during these last two weeks:

I learned that cancer treatment is making really rapid progress, and that some of our fears of the disease and its treatment are based on the past, and that while it's no picnic, it's manageable.

I've learned that Wichita has a remarkably good treatment facility in the Cancer Center of Kansas.

I've learned that cancer isn't necessarily a synonym for death.

I've learned that this latest stuff has no relation to the bladder cancer that I had. I just happened to be standing next to the cancer tree and got a double dose.

I've learned that EARLY treatment is a MUST. If you think something is wrong, it probably is. CHECK IT OUT!

I've learned that vitamins and healthy eating could help.

I've learned that knowing is better than not knowing. Once I learned what I have and what the treatment would be, I was able to let go of the fear and concentrate on the cure.

I've learned that I like the sound of that word more each day.

Cure.

We Could Learn a Few Valuable Lessons from Our Canine Friends

AUGUST 16, 2001 : The other day I was petting my dog, Ranger, and he was nuzzling me and studying me with those quizzical brown eyes of his as if to say, "Everything is going to be all right," and I got to thinking about what a neat thing God did when he gave mankind dogkind.

He must have known that humans were going to need steadfast, loyal and dedicated companions, so he invented dogs.

He made them soft and hairy so they were easy to pet and caress, then he made them loving and affectionate so humans starved for those two qualities could always find them in a faithful dog. He then made sure that the dog was stalwart and alert, and gave him a territorial sense so that he could always be on the lookout for danger and protect his master.

He imbedded in every dog's personality an abiding joy that knows no boundaries. When a dog spies his master coming home after an absence, his heart swells with such happiness that he has to run and leap and bark with unbridled enthusiasm. There is nothing on earth so uplifting as a happy dog greeting his favorite human.

God, being so wise, didn't stop there. He knew, I think, that humans can sometimes be unfaithful to each other and untrue to their promises, so he implanted in every dog's psyche a powerful strain of faithfulness.

Dogs are the most faithful creatures alive. Once a dog gives you his love, nothing can persuade him to leave you. Not cruelty or meanness or neglect can turn him against you. He will lick the hand that strikes him, return to the owner that abandons him or die trying to find his way back. You can be a dishonest, weak and thoroughly reprehensible person, void of all human friendship, and still your dog will be faithful to you until his life leaves him.

After creating the near-perfect creature, God obviously pondered his work and decided that, along with all the other traits, a dog should be intelligent. It is clear that he felt that dogs should possess an instinct that would keep them from harm and allow them the tools to help their master stay out of harm's way. They bark when danger abounds. There are countless stories of dogs alerting their owners of a nighttime fire or helping to save a drowning child. In such instances, they are courageous and persistent in their duty and true to their calling.

God also made dogs helpful. They help hunt, find drug smugglers, do search and rescue, herd cattle and sheep, guide the blind and guard humans and property. Teach them tricks, and they will delight you with their ability to do your bidding and do it to the point of exhaustion.

It's evident that God knew also that humans are sometimes hard-hearted, so he made puppies cute enough to melt hard hearts and so irresistible that even the most reluctant of us want to give them a home.

I can only assume that God was fully aware of the great and gracious gift he was bestowing on the world he'd created, for he is all-wise. But somehow I can't help but wonder if he knew the miracle of happiness that dogs would bring to children, old folks, widowers and retired guys like me.

I can shut my eyes and imagine our world without a lot of things, but I can't imagine the world without the warm, loving comfort of my dog on a cold and lonely night. I can also imagine how much better the world would be if we humans could learn a few traits from dogs.

We could use a dog's sense of loyalty and devotion and faithfulness and duty. We could stand to be little more demonstrative to those we love and cherish, and a little less subdued in our expressions of adoration to our loved ones.

I don't dare question God's wisdom, but I can't help wishing that he'd given dogs a longer life span. Most of the dogs I've known deserved to live longer than they did. The loss of a beloved dog is a pain that you never get over, triggering memories that last a lifetime and bringing tears and sorrow in a flash of recollection.

Maybe that's what God had in mind all along.

You Mold the Clay That Is a Child's Soul

AUGUST 23, 2001 : We adults should be ashamed of ourselves. I say that because I've been reflecting on how it comes to pass that perfectly innocent little kids grow up to be less-than-perfect adults. There's nothing so pure and innocent as a 6-year-old. At 6, the little person is square with the world. Days are filled with such simple pleasures as playing ball, playing with dolls, petting the dog, digging in the dirt, laughing at the wonder of a June bug and waiting for story time at night.

Six-year-olds are still honest; they still look up to Mom and Dad as the most important people in the world. They chase butterflies in the summer and build snowmen in the winter with a bubbling enthusiasm and innocence that exudes sheer joy.

They trust everybody, believe in magic and imagine all things are possible. They do not know how to have bad thoughts about anyone. They get over being mad almost instantly. If they get hurt, they get over it quickly and forgive the person who hurt them. They are as near to perfect as a human being can be. I liken them to soft potter's clay.

The clay is still warm and pliable.

Sometime between the ages of 7 and 10, the sweetness and innocence start to erode. The world begins to take its toll on the young ones. They learn that Mom and Dad aren't perfect after all. They discover that maybe they were misled about Santa and tooth fairies and such. They learn that grownups lie. They learn about broken promises, deceit,

selfishness and disappointment.

Their faith in adult role models, which seemed so solid, begins to disintegrate, and they seek new role models among their peers. They learn to use profanity. Still possessing a child's curiosity, they explore the adult world around them, finding access to all of the adult ills: pornography, violence, alcohol, tobacco and drugs.

By the time they have become teenagers, the pattern is set. Innocence for the most part is lost. The child will never again be pure, and cynicism, distrust, disillusionment and sarcasm will define the personality of this once near-perfect human being.

And the clay begins to harden.

It's fairly common practice to blame "bad kids" for many of our problems, but what about bad adults? Adults make the TV shows and movies that glorify irresponsible sex and violence. Adults make the pornography, import and distribute the drugs, and sell this filth to the youth for profit.

Adults get the divorces that destroy homes and shatter belief systems. Adults break the promises, utter the profanities and demonstrate the deceit and dishonesty that prevail all around us. Adults abandon their families, beat their spouses, abuse their children and, by their actions, teach prejudice and hatred.

Not kids. Adults.

Adults are the potters who put the final imprints in the clay that is a child's immortal soul. When these final imprints are impressed, they can't be changed without some life-altering, significant emotional event.

For now the clay is permanently hardened.

I'm not saying that all kids turn out bad, or that there are no good adults. I am saying that we'd be better off if somehow we could live our lives more like that 6-year-old and less like adults.

What a wonderful world it would be if we could all become 6-year-olds again and somehow retain the ability to trust, to be truthful and enthusiastic, and to not nurse our hurts and grudges past a good nap or recess time. What if we could grow up that way, and teach our children that perfect innocence is the way to live, and prove that we are truly deserving of a 6-year-old's faith and confidence and devotion?

Next time you get to talk to a 6-year-old, look closely. You will never see a more perfect or innocent human being. And remember:

You are the potter.

MADDIE & GRANDPAW

You Choose the Attitude That You Carry through Life

SEPTEMBER 6, 2001 : "You've got a great attitude, so I know you'll whip this cancer thing," a friend of mine said recently. "Yeah," I thought to myself. "What's attitude got to do with it?"

Later, as I began thinking about it, I decided maybe my friend was right. Maybe I needed all the medical help I could get and a good dose of great attitude to boot.

Frankly, at the time my attitude wasn't so great. I was starting to feel a little snake-bit, as they say out in Texas, and though I was keeping up appearances, my attitude was in pretty sorry shape.

That set me to thinking about attitudes in general.

"What is a great attitude, or what is a bad attitude?" I pondered to myself. (I ponder a lot these days — a sign, I'm sure, of advancing age.) I finally came up with these thoughts about attitudes that I'd like to share with you in the hopes that you will agree. If you don't agree, don't tell me 'cause I pondered so dad-gummed hard on these I'd have my feelings hurt!

A bad attitude usually includes these traits:

Pessimism. You just know that everything is going to come out wrong. Consequently, you expect the worst, and, sure enough, the worst always seems to happen.

Distrust. You don't really trust anyone with your money, your ideas or your future. You think everyone is only out for himself and can't be counted on to do right by you.

Envy. You find it hard to pay others a compliment or congratulate them because, secretly, you think their accomplishments weren't deserved or maybe should have happened to you instead of them.

Indecision. You find it hard to make life choices and tend to put them off for some future time when, you tell yourself, it'll be easier.

Blame. You tend to feel that others are the reason you haven't done as well as you'd like. It's the "I would have succeeded if only so-and-so hadn't happened" syndrome. You are sure that your misfortune was beyond your control and caused by some outside force.

Anger. You find yourself blowing up at what you imagine to be bad service, or a slight by a friend or relative. You tend to carry grudges long after such an incident, and you recount that anger to all who will listen, for it lives inside you and seems fresh every day.

Loneliness. You don't seem to have many friends, and you find yourself alone more often than not. Unfortunately, while some of the above traits are imagined, this one probably is not, because people don't like to be around those who constantly exude a bad attitude.

A good attitude, I think, includes these traits:

Enthusiasm. Enthusiasm for all things that engage you. You approach life cheerfully and optimistically with high-outcome expectations, and you feel that no matter what comes up, you will be able to handle it effectively.

Warmth. A good attitude will cause you

to put other folks around you at ease. You manage that by being genuinely interested in them and their thoughts, and by being as good a listener as you are a talker.

Confidence. Your confidence in yourself and your abilities is strong, but not so strong that it becomes cockiness or conceit. You know your own talents and are aware of your shortcomings enough that you are confident of your abilities, or lack of them, in any situation.

Positiveness. You try to find the good in all people and circumstances. You recognize that good exists in all things, as does bad, but you choose to dwell on the good. You bite your tongue when you have negative thoughts about another person.

Beliefs. You possess strong beliefs about your principles, your family and your ethics. You don't incessantly foist these beliefs on those around you, nor do you criticize those who hold different concepts dear. You tolerate their beliefs and adhere to yours without being insufferable about them.

Respect. You respect other people's dignity, reputation and privacy. You maintain a healthy respect for the things that are out of your control.

Energy. A good attitude promotes high energy and a zest for life that carries you through with an upbeat outlook that draws people and success to you.

The absolutely neat thing about attitudes is that you can actually choose which kind you're going to maintain. I think it's possible, with some work, to have a great one as opposed to a bad one by simply deciding to adopt it.

I'm working on mine right now!

Those Who Attacked Us Deserve Swift, Sure Justice

SEPTEMBER 27, 2001 : On Tuesday morning, September 11, like you, I woke up to the news of the World Trade Center tragedy. My first thought was of my daughter, Melissa, my grandbabies, Max and Maddie, and my son-in-law, Todd.

Like hundreds of thousands of other concerned parents, brothers, sisters, friends and relatives, I tried to call, only to be notified that "all circuits are busy." I must have tried 20 times and still couldn't get through, my anxiety mounting with every beep of the keypad.

You see, Melissa and Todd live only about 20 blocks from the World Trade Center, and the kids' schools are even closer. The planes hit the towers at just about the time Todd would have been walking them to school.

In between my frantic dialing, friends began calling to ask if Melissa and Todd were OK, and of course I had no answer. Then - FINALLY!! -Melissa managed to get through.

She was OK. Todd was OK and had been called in to his anchor desk at WCBS, Channel 2, to report on the chaos. The school had just notified Melissa that everything was fine, that they had shut down the school and would watch the kids until she could come and get them. She was on her way, she said, and did not know for sure how to get there because cabs were not running and there was pandemonium in the streets as New Yorkers became aware of the disaster.

I breathed a sigh of relief and went to my doctor's appointment.

That afternoon I called to make sure Melissa had gotten home safely and to see how the grandkids were handling the awful scene, which they could see from the window of their 48th-floor apartment.

I received the most animated description of the situation you can imagine from 11-year-old Max. "Two giant planes, taken over by some really bad men, crashed into the world empire building! Both the buildings have fallen down and people are running down the street, and my teacher was scared and so was I, and there's smoke coming down, and it's just awful!"

Maddie's turn. "Mike, just like Max said, it's awful." Then she said something that has stuck with me ever since. She described it in 8-year-olds' words. "Mike, it looks to me like New York City got its two front teeth knocked out."

To her those twin towers resembled two giant front teeth. Now, just like when she lost her two front teeth, only gaps remain. I've heard all manner of descriptions about the aftermath of this horrible event, and none struck me as so profound as my little granddaughter's impression. I will never forget her tone of voice and the profound simplicity of her statement.

Like all Americans, I will also never forget the images of those planes ripping into those buildings.

At this writing, our government has not responded with much more than words, though I'm sure we will. Like all Americans, I'm angry and want swift and just punishment to those who killed so many people and put my family in harm's way. I hope that the justice will come quickly.

And I hope that we have the will to suspend our sensibilities to civil liberties and rule of law when it comes to tracking and eliminating these vermin, for I believe that they use our laws and fear of violating civil rights against us to carry out their terror. I can't see as how they have the rights to such once we know their involvement.

I hope that our politicians will stand as united as they have been thus far, and I hope that our fellow citizens will remember the mistakes of World War II and not persecute the innocent, peaceful Muslims in this country. I believe most of them are loyal, law-abiding citizens who are as outraged as the rest of us.

I hope that our intelligence agencies are up to the task of ensuring that this can never happen again by shoring up our ability to know our enemy. I hope that we will never again be lulled into a false sense of security and become so lax that this can happen again.

Most of all, I hope that the sense of patriotism that is sweeping the nation will stick this time, and that we will never need a tragic event like this, or a war, to trigger it again.

Like you, I pray for our president and wish him Godspeed in his mission to find and punish the cowards and zealots who brought such pain to so many innocent people and knocked out our "two front teeth."

Let's Hope That, This Time, Patriotism Stays in Vogue

OCTOBER 25, 2001 : All of a sudden, it's OK to be patriotic again. I'm writing this from my motor home on a trip across the great Southwest, and signs of patriotism are everywhere: the American flag painted across the back of trucks headed west on I-40, antenna flags flapping in the breeze from cars, SUVs and pickups.

The words "God Bless America" are plastered on billboards up and down the interstate or spray-painted on everything from bridges to Indian jewelry vendors' roadside huts in Arizona. Radio stations are playing patriotic music and airing promotions that uplift patriotism and love of country.

Overnight, it seems, it has become politically incorrect to criticize the president or the government. Politicians who once could find nothing good to say about President Bush are standing in line to praise him and to support the programs he needs to fight terrorism. Media commentators who a few weeks ago openly questioned the president's ability are now talking about his strong leadership. The late-night comedians who derided not only President Bush but the government are fresh out of material.

I love it!

I love my country, and I love the fact that my country loves itself again.

What I don't understand, though, is why it takes a tragedy like what happened on September 11, or the Gulf War of 10 years ago, to trigger this patriotic fervor.

After the Gulf War, you'll recall, we "blessed America," flew the flag, wore patriotic T-shirts and sang patriotic songs for a time, then slowly but surely returned to our old ways. Partisan political wrangling, smart-aleck comedians and ultra-liberal media commentators were back in style, and it was no longer cool to be openly patriotic. Anyone who stood for American might, or military responses to terrorists, was considered a Neanderthal with a 1940s mentality.

We endured embassy bombings, downed airliners and terrorist threats and responded only when the polls showed that lobbing a few missiles at Afghanistan would be politically popular.

Politicians were busily dismantling our ability to gather intelligence against outside threats. The CIA and FBI were systematically handcuffed and rendered virtually impotent by many of the same folks who are now wondering where our intelligence capabilities went. Movies, books and television portrayed the government as some kind of sinister monster bent on depriving its citizens of freedoms, and several movies pictured the president as an out-and-out crook.

Patriotism was out, and cynicism was in.

I hope that this time it takes. I hope that as we deal with bio-terrorism, bomb threats and the loss of much of our freedom to move about conveniently, we will realize how blessed we are, and have been.

I hope it will never again be out of fashion to display the flag, or to pledge allegiance, or to play a patriotic song on the radio.

I hope that the CIA and FBI are given the power to gather the intelligence necessary to identify and bring to justice those who would do us harm, and that we are never again reticent about using our might to respond to any country that would take away our way of life.

I hope we stay patriotic.

I stood on the edge of the Grand Canyon the other day, gazing out across that beautiful landscape and marveling at the breathtaking majesty of this country and all the bounty it provides and, I'm not ashamed to say, was moved to tears. The words to Lee Greenwood's "God Bless the USA" kept running through my mind as yet another semi roared by with "God Bless America" emblazoned on the side.

Maybe this time it will take.

TV News Could Learn a Lot from Ernie Pyle

November 1, 2001 : I gotta get this off my chest. I'm a media guy. I believe fervently that a free society MUST have a free media in order to keep those in government from manipulating the public. I believe that media bias is possible, so it's healthy to have liberal outlets and conservative outlets in media so both points of view are available. But lately, I think we've gone too far.

A friend of mine, who shares the view I'm about to impart, summed it up the other day when he sighed and said, "Where's Ernie Pyle when you need him?"

Ernie Pyle was the Pulitzer Prize-winning roving reporter for the Scripps-Howard newspaper chain during World War II. He wrote a simple, down-to-earth column from the European battlefronts that was syndicated in more than 200 newspapers across the country. But he never disclosed the whereabouts of troops before a battle.

In short, he managed to keep America informed without endangering our Army or relating sensitive information that could be used against our forces by the enemy.

Edward R. Murrow did the same in his famous radio broadcasts from "somewhere on the European front." They and others like them seemed to work in harmony with the war effort without sacrificing the public's right to know what their country was doing.

Where the heck are they or men like them now?

With the proliferation of 24-hour cable news channels, we've spawned a whole new news genre that is a hungry monster. The fact is, there's only so much news to impart in a given day, and some days there's not near enough to fill a 24-hour, seven-day schedule. To remedy this, cable news channels in particular, and the big four networks to some degree, have added shows dealing with the analysis of news.

I call them the "what if-ers."

It's these guys' job to fill time with endless speculation about whatever little news there might be, massage it every which way, spin it, dissect it and speculate on it. All manner of experts are called upon to offer their opinions, which many times come off as fact instead of opinion. If there is a hot topic, such as the Gary Condit matter or more recently the September 11 attacks and subsequent anthrax scare, then it will be bantered about incessantly on these shows and repeated ad infinitum.

Then there is the age-old competition between these outlets to break the story first. Unfortunately, the line between breaking the story and making the story has become blurred. The talking analysts raise the "what if," and sometimes the "what if" becomes the news.

Within a week after the September 11 tragedy, the cable shows were speculating on bio-terrorism and our preparedness to handle an anthrax attack. Special after special showed how it could be done. Then, almost as a self-fulfilling prophecy, someone did it.

I'm convinced that those shows played a huge part in alerting either some goofball over here to the fact that he could make waves and maybe be famous, or at worst, some terrorist cell that we are most scared of bio-warfare. In either case, the speculation could have actually helped cause the events.

Now the news channels are speculating about how a small-pox attack would be even more devastating than anthrax, and frankly I'm worried that the publicity about our lack of preparedness will set some other nutcase loose on a mission to make the news.

The other thing that sickens me is watching a briefing or news conference by our government officials and watching reporters disintegrate into a pack of howling hyenas, trying to get the officials to disclose some information that our government considers classified. When they're told politely that the information is not going to be given out, they continue to ask the same question over and over, and get pouty when they can't worm it out of the officials.

Every channel apparently has a cadre of retired generals who then take the air to tell what the officials didn't. Net result, I'm afraid, is way too much information flowing to the enemy.

Is it possible that these news-hungry monsters have become a tool the terrorists have learned to manipulate?

Like my friend said: Where is Ernie Pyle when we need him?

We Can't Let Fear Warp the Way We See Others

NOVEMBER 8, 2001 : The September 11 attack hit close to home. Again. I was talking to an old and dear friend of mine, and he shared his story, which prompted me to think about what has happened from an entirely different perspective.

Hanna Sahleyeh, my friend, is in the incentive travel business in Dallas. Over the past 30 years he has built one of the most successful companies of its type in the United States. He handles incentive trips for GE, Southland Life and many other major corporations. As such, he handled trips for KFDI and our group of radio stations for nearly 30 years.

His company is noted for outstanding service and attention to detail, and in all the years he dealt with us, we never had a bad trip. We traveled with our advertisers all over the world. Over those years he became a close friend as well as a business associate. He is a friend defined by his intuitive wisdom, deep caring and graciousness.

Hanna came to this country as a young man from Jerusalem. His Palestinian family was poor, and he had to leave to better himself. After working in Turkey and Italy arranging military tours for our armed forces, he went to work in the travel industry with his uncle, who had already established a large, well-recognized incentive travel business in the United States.

An intense apprenticeship taught him enough to strike out on his own, and over the next several years he grew his company into a multimillion-dollar concern that handled tens of thousands of trips per year. I well remember when, in the midst of all that, Hanna was studying for his American citizenship exam and how hard he worked, and how proud he was when he passed it with a perfect score.

As his company grew, so did his family. Because he was successful, he became the sole support of his father, two brothers and a sister. He married a beautiful girl from his country and they had two lovely young girls, now college age. Over those same years Hanna invested wisely, paid his taxes, contributed hundreds of thousands of dollars to charities, and enriched his employees by giving them shares of his business and providing extraordinary benefits and salaries. His most recent triumph, and sorrow, he says, was when his oldest daughter went away to Vanderbilt University to begin her college education.

I can safely say that Hanna is one of the finest individuals I've ever known. He is as American as I am and probably appreciates our country more than most of us who've been able to take its bounty for granted all our lives. I know from many conversations with him that he would literally lay down his life for this country, and I believe no one is kinder to his fellow man.

Consider how his life has changed since September 11th. First, within hours after the tragedy, bookings that his company had worked on for months began to cancel. Millions of dollars in cancellations occurred within days. His firm's investment in setting up these trips cannot be recouped. While some of the planned trips will be rescheduled to places in the United States, the loss to Hanna's company will be immense.

Because he and his family are Arab in appearance, they have already encountered the suspicious looks, the questioning of the name and no doubt much more scrutiny on the very airlines to which he's fed so much business over the years. He says he's glad for the extra security, even though it's uncomfortable, but it hurts him deeply when he considers the ramifications for his family.

He figures he can subsist through the downturn in his business and is proud of the fact that no employee has been laid off and that his staff is creatively responding to the challenge. His most fervent wish that Osama bin Laden be brought to justice.

He says he prays for that every night.

Hanna is just one example of hundreds of thousands of Arab Americans who, by their productivity and devotion to America, make us a greater nation.

We must not repeat the mistakes we made with Japanese Americans in World War II by becoming a nation unable to discern the difference between loyal, patriotic Americans and a few fanatical, warped zealots.

That would be the worst terror.

Life, Love, Family, Friends: Give Thanks for Them All

NOVEMBER 22, 2001 : It occurs to me as my family gathers for Thanksgiving today that we, as a nation, truly should be very thankful.

It also is plain to me that I personally owe an abundance of thanks for the many blessings that have come my way these past several years.

I sat for a while the other day on my deck, watching the golden and auburn leaves trickle down into the yard, the squirrels busy gathering their winter provisions, and thought about the things for which I am grateful. I was overwhelmed at the number of things that came to me that cause a sense of gratitude. I share them with you today, in no particular order, in the hope that you will start your own list on this day of thanksgiving.

I am thankful for the adversity that has befallen me these past two years, for it has taught me how precious and how fragile life really is. The loss of loved ones, the bouts with two kinds of cancer and the resolution of those medical challenges in a way that gives me more years to be on this earth, I believe, have made me a better person. I now feel more compassion for my fellow man, and am not so certain that I alone am in control of my well-being.

I am thankful for my children, for they have shown me, above all else, the essence of a life well-intended. I see in their faces and actions that the values and ideas that their mother and I imparted have come to fruition, and I know as I watch them raise their own families that those years of work and nurturing were not in vain.

I also am most thankful for my grandchildren, for they have given me a chance to relive my kids' childhoods, and to perhaps make up for the omissions of togetherness dictated by a demanding career and workaholic pace that kept me away from the important things.

I am thankful for my friends, for they have enveloped me with a special warmth and sense of belonging that have kept me in good humor in times when nothing seemed worthy of laughter. They coaxed smiles and then laughter from a guy who thought he'd never truly live again, and steadfastly refused to let me wallow in self-pity.

I am thankful for the medical profession (Boy, am I!), for it has taught me that there is always hope, and that new advances are being made daily which can and will prolong life and improve its quality. Diseases that once brought only suffering and death are now in retreat, and new discoveries that will expand our longevity loom on the near and far horizons.

I am thankful that I live in Wichita, for it has taught me the value of service to one's community. Serving others with whatever talent you have produces a warm inner glow and an irreplaceable sense of pride and self-worth.

Most of all, on this Thanksgiving Day, I am grateful for the ability to love and be loved. I once thought that I'd never again be capable of feeling anything but sorrow, and now I know better.

It must be that God so values love above all else that he replenishes our supply of it even when it seems the farthest removed. I know now that love doesn't end with death or separation, but continues and even grows.

So as we bow our heads today to give thanks, I will offer grace for my good fortune, for my kids and their kids, my friends, my community, the miracle of science, those whom I have loved, and for the fact that I have been blessed with a new love who renews my desire to live life to its fullest.

For all of that abundance, I am most truly grateful.

OL' MIKE AND PEGI ON THEIR HONEYMOON

When You Look Like a Cue Ball, You Learn All About Humility

NOVEMBER 29, 2001 : I'll begin with an open apology to all the bald guys in Wichita! I am truly sorry that I ever felt smug because I had hair and you didn't.

Oh, I never said anything about it out loud, but secretly, whenever I was in your presence with my hair intact and yours gone, I'll admit I felt, well . . . superior.

Now that I've lived among you as a bald guy since my chemo treatments, now that I've walked a mile in your shoes, I am truly repentant of my holier-than-thou attitude.

You see, if the truth were known, I've always had a fear of being bald. My danged hair was always as fine as cat fur, and I worried for years that it would disappear by the time I was 30. It didn't, but it got thin enough to worry the heck out of me. I studied hair transplant ads, thinking I might need the knowledge someday. I was inwardly pleased when they announced the Rogaine breakthrough, thinking that in case I actually did lose it all, there might be a medical solution.

By the time I was 40, it was evident that I was going to retain enough hair to still have to comb it, and it was then that I became an insensitive hair supremacist, cocky and coolly indifferent to my friends who were molting with age.

I made bald jokes (*You look like Yul Brynner on steroids; Can't see your eyes for the glare*). I was merciless in my superiority, for I had HAIR, you see, and they didn't!

I can confess this now that I've lived among the bald, for I am currently one of you! I, too, have watched my hair come out in clumps. I, too, have seen the look on people's faces as they try to avert their eyes from my shiny dome; I, too, have looked in the mirror to see a scalded chicken staring back where once there was a curly mass of thinning but clearly substantial hair.

I, too, like the Gipper with his amputated leg, have awakened in the night thinking my hair was still there. I, too, have instinctively reached for the brush only to be cruelly reminded that it is no longer needed. I, like you, have covered my shiny pate with everything from a ball cap to a motorcycle scarf, trying to hide my shame.

Slowly but surely, the realization dawns on you that YOU HAVE NO HAIR! Then you get angry. (*That's right, I'm bald! Wanna make something of it?*) Gradually, you come to accept it, and outside of a few insensitive friends (as I was) making jokes and women rubbing your scalp, you get used to it.

Fortunately, my bald experience comes at a time when it's fashionable to be bald. Michael Jordan, Andre Agassi, Jesse Ventura, Bruce Willis and a host of others have shaved their heads and started a trend that is sweeping the nation. We bald guys can follow along and for a time, while the trend lasts, can say we were pioneers in the movement.

I've also learned that there are definite positives to being bald. You don't have to fool with your hair in the morning; there are no barber bills; women do like to rub your scalp for some twisted, weird reason; and you don't have to spend money on hair care products. It has its advantages!

For me, it's been a revelation. Most of the bald guys I know got that way gradually over the years, so that they actually began to look distinguished and intelligent. The hair gods decided to get my attention by taking it all away in a week or so, after the first chemo treatment. I look anything but distinguished and intelligent. (Can you say *cue ball*?)

They say my hair will come back after a while, but my life as a bald guy has taught me some lessons:

1. Don't take your hair for granted.

2. Don't be smug 'cause you have it and someone else doesn't.

3. There is life after hair.

4. It's kind of nice to have weird, twisted women rub your scalp!

So, bald guys, please accept my apology, and I'll see you at the next BGOWSG (Bald Guys of Wichita Support Group) meeting!

If There's Radio in Heaven, Willie Wheelchair's on It

DECEMBER 13, 2001 : Willie Heatwole was an all-night dispatcher at the sheriff's office when our paths first crossed in 1966.

I was signing on the station (KFDI) at 5 a.m. at the time, and Willie would call around 5:15 and request a record. He also began asking me what it took to become a disc jockey. We got asked that a lot in those days, and not wanting to hurt his feelings, I suppose, I tried to discourage him from even thinking about it.

"You need a first-class radio-telephone license," I told him. Back then, the FCC required a station as powerful as KFDI to have an operator with such a license. I had mine, as did all of the "ranch hands" at the station.

To get one, you had to go to school for six to eight weeks and pass a very difficult series of tests, and it was rather costly. The nearest school was in Dallas. I explained all of that to Willie and suggested that he was probably better off where he was.

He heard me, but apparently paid no attention. Eight weeks later he appeared at the station, announcing that he'd obtained his first-class license, quit his job at the sheriff's office and was ready to go to work.

I was impressed with his determination, even more so when I learned that he was confined to a wheelchair. (He'd never mentioned it in all his phone calls to the station.) To make a long story shorter, Willie dubbed himself Willie Wheelchair and became a ranch hand that day, and was still one 35 years later.

He was there as a single AM country radio station grew to become the largest country music-formatted chain in the country. He was there as other ranch hands came and went. He was there as country music grew into a giant industry. He was still there when at last Great Empire Broadcasting, the station's parent company, was sold to the Journal Broadcast Group.

He had strong opinions about all of that and frequently stepped on toes as he expressed those opinions to any and all who would listen. He and another of our air personalities, Buddy Nichols, used to shock our listeners by getting into knock-down, drag-out arguments on the air. They sounded like they were going to come to blows, but they were the best of friends up until Buddy's death a few years ago.

The only time I ever saw Willie emotional was at Buddy's funeral. I remember him rolling out of the little church where the service was held, head bowed and tears streaming down his cheeks.

Willie worked full time at the station for several years, but his deteriorating health finally forced him into part-time status. He spent countless days in the hospital getting skin grafts and such, but he always acted like it was nothing. He'd bounce back after one of those hospital stays with a chipper attitude that belied his handicap and poor condition. He nearly made his co-workers forget that he was struggling every day to do what we did effortlessly.

I've thought a lot about Willie in the past

few days. That car wreck so many years ago robbed him of the use of his legs but couldn't take his spirit. Those many trips to the hospital usurped his strength but couldn't curb his enthusiasm for his family, his listeners, the station and life in general.

We managers could scold him and discipline him, but we couldn't keep him from speaking his mind on and off the air. As his boss, I had to fuss at him several times over the years, but I always secretly admired his loyalty and devotion to the station, and to his listeners.

I don't know whether there is a radio station in heaven, but if there is, I'll bet Willie has already convinced the angel in charge that the station can't do without him, and that he walked, instead of rolled, into the studio, and that he and Buddy Nichols are already quarreling on the air. And I'll give you two to one that he opened his show up there with these words: "This is Willie Wheelchair and I'm PROUD to have YOU listenin'."

We were proud, too, Willie.

Proud to have known you.

THE KFDI RANCH HANDS – 1972

Imagine If Santa Claus Caught
the Corporate Urge to Merge

DECEMBER 27, 2001 : Given all that has transpired in the business world this last year, you can imagine what would happen if Santa Claus functioned like some of our corporate moguls. I mean, with just a little flight of fancy, you can imagine reading in the business publications the following:

Because of a slower-than-predicted Christmas season, and because of an anticipated slowdown this Easter, merger talks between Santa Claus and the Easter Bunny are under way.

Sources confirm that Santa was despondent after this Christmas season and that the North Pole is dangerously overstocked with toys that didn't get on children's wish lists at expected levels. The net result, according to the sources, is that a panic-stricken Santa contacted the Easter Bunny yesterday, and the two CEOs met over lunch to discuss the merger.

Reportedly, the issues that were discussed in detail had to do with the possible efficiencies that could result from the consolidation, and centered on how the retirement plans of some 250,000 elves employed at the North Pole could be accelerated in the event of a downsizing.

The two also supposedly discussed which of them would be the chairman, and which would be the chief operations officer. They reportedly agreed to engage the accounting firm of Arthur Andersen to assist in valuations for both entities, citing the firm's forward-thinking creativity in such matters.

While no decision was apparently reached on who would lead the proposed new operation, insiders are betting on the bunny, who has the edge on Santa in knowledge of technology and is actually using a cell phone and laptop to monitor his production. Santa, on the other hand, is known to detest anything wireless, and has admitted that he hates XBoxes and Cubes and that little kids who request them next year are likely to get a box of Legos instead.

Those closest to Santa say the executive is merely 'tired' from the season and won't give control to the bunny unless pressured by the board of directors.

If this kind of thing happens, I can see all kinds of problems. Start with the fact that there would be a huge monopoly created. This would give Democrats heartburn and upset stomachs and worry Republicans to death trying to figure out how to give the new outfit a sizable tax break.

Next thing you know, when little kids try to call Santa, they would get an automated answering system.(Press 1 for Santa, 2 for the Easter Bunny.)

In the rush for consolidation "efficiencies," 30 percent of both companies' work forces could be laid off. If you figure that the Easter Bunny employs over 2 million egg-laying rabbits, 30 percent would be 600,000 out-of-work rabbits, and 30 percent of 250,000 elves would be 75,000 out-of-work elves.

Given what rabbits do when they're idle and given the sudden influx of little pointed-ear people who have no job skills other than making toys, why, the country would be in dire straits. We'd be up to our elbows in rabbits and elves before we knew it.

After the layoffs, the next thing you know would be the announcement that Christmas and Easter would be combined into one holiday, thereby offending all of the union folks and the civil servants, not to mention millions of Christians around the world. This would produce untold numbers of court challenges and strikes, which could further damage the fragile economy.

Children would receive Easter baskets laden with eggs, and Legos and XBoxes would be delivered by giant rabbits bred for efficiency. Santa's sled would be retired to a company museum, and the reindeer would be forced into early retirement.

About the only good thing you'd see come out of this would be a "strong buy" recommendation from the Wall Street brokerage firms.

I don't know whether this can happen or not, but just to be on the safe side, I'm calling my broker!

Battling Cancer Can Make You Appreciate Good Health

JANUARY 3, 2002 : Cancer has taught me a profound life lesson.

I wish I could have learned it intellectually. Instead, I learned it, you might say, the hard way. The lesson? I learned how important good health is to our quality of life.

Plain and simple, the absence of good health this past year, and the prospects brought to mind by the word *cancer*, drove home to me how singularly important good health is.

OK, I'll admit that I, like most of you, could grasp the importance of good health, a good diet, regular exercise, etc. But it wasn't until I faced the prospect of a life-threatening disease and the possibility of never feeling good again that I began to understand how important health is to every other thing in life.

I also began thinking about the ingredients to good health that are within our control. Looking back over my experience this past year, I'd have to say that these ingredients, or keys, didn't prevent me from having a health crisis, but they have sure played a part in my recovery.

Happiness is a key to good health. Without the ability to work and play and to experience life's pleasures, happiness eludes us. It is important, then, to reach out for happiness and to work at identifying the things that produce happiness in the face of ill health.

Enthusiasm is a key to good health. When you don't feel well, being enthusiastic about anything somehow seems impossible. But enthusiasm is the zest that makes bad health an obstacle to be overcome rather than a one-way trip.

Hope is a key to good health. It is hard to have hope without good health, but I believe that it is essential to good health to have hope. Without hope, a person is prone to give up and perhaps not be willing to undertake the sometimes painful and strenuous path back to good health. Hope, in fact, might be the only way to regain good health once it is lost.

I've thought a lot about how in the world I could get cancer in the first place. I don't smoke or drink, and outside of a not-so-healthy diet and not a lot of exercise these past 10 years, I considered myself pretty darn healthy. It wasn't until my darkest time that bad health descended upon me. In other words, it came when hope and enthusiasm and happiness had departed.

It followed, then, that if somehow I could regain those three keys, then perhaps I could regain that ever-so-precious gift of good health.

I won't bore you with the details, but I found my lost happiness at my doorstep, in the love of my family and friends, and my lost enthusiasm in the promise the future holds for love and a new life, and I found hope in the knowledge that we live in a wondrous time when the medical profession is capable of marvelous healing and cures.

At this writing, I still don't know whether I'm cured. I live with the knowledge that all cancer patients have, that "it" could return someday. However, I face it with a prevailing happiness, an unquenchable enthusiasm and eternal hope.

Someone wished me Happy New Year the other day, and my first reaction was to say that 2001 was a rotten year. Now, I'm not so sure, for it was during that year that I regained what I'd lost the previous year, and that I learned to appreciate what a marvelous gift we have in good health. I carry that lesson into the promise of 2002 and beyond.

I reckon that's as good as it gets.

Uncle Sam's Charity Is Well-Intentioned but Misplaced

JANUARY 17, 2002 : I was watching one of those infernal news shows the other night, and the lead story was about how the families of the victims of the September 11th attacks were mighty unhappy about the government's formula for distributing the several million dollars set aside for those folks.

It reminded me of why the government ought to stay the heck out of the charity business and leave that to us citizens.

As I understand it, the government appropriated those funds as a way of helping both the victims' families and the airlines. Those who accept the money must agree not to sue the airlines. The rationale is that providing them the money compensates them for giving up their right to sue for damages.

The same legislation that provides the funds limits the damages that anyone who does sue can collect.

You might say that the use of our taxes in this manner is an attempt by the government to be charitable to the families and to a beleaguered industry. I suppose it all made sense to those birds up in Washington. Spread a little money around (to them, this is pocket change) and help the little people and protect the big folks.

Trouble is, almost no one is happy! The victims' families are up in arms because some will get more of this bird nest than others because of the distribution formula. Firefighters' families, for instance, will apparently receive less because the amount of their public pensions and insurance settlements will be deducted from their federal allot-ments. Widows are calling news conferences and complaining on national news programs that it's all unfair.

The airlines are upset, because the millions they've received don't bail them out adequately. The trial lawyers are incensed at the limits placed on damages that can be collected from suits. Victims from other tragedies are wondering where THEIR compensation is. Taxpayers are starting to wonder if this is a good use of the billions we send to Washington every year.

In short, what seemed like a good idea in the aftermath of September 11th will most likely turn into a political cesspool, awash in greed and good old American finger-pointing, and might backfire on the politicians who thought it would be a sure-fire winner on Election Day.

I think it's a dangerous precedent. Uncle Sam is already up to his fanny in the charity business, and this concept could put him in up to his little white goatee!

What happens when the next terrorist attack occurs? What happens to the victims of the next big tornado or snowstorm? What about the folks who lose a wage earner in a tragic car wreck? What about the victims' families in Oklahoma City? What about the next big industry that gets their pants sued off?

The fact is that we Americans don't need the bureaucracy to take care of our own. We contributed more than a billion and a half dollars to the victims' families in the same neighbors-helping-neighbors spirit that has defined our country from the beginning.

The government would be of far greater service to those families by seeing to it that the contributions are actually distributed instead of being hung up in red tape, as much of the funds apparently still are. It makes perfect sense, in this instance, for the government to set limits on collectable damages, as the airlines are perilously close to financial collapse and we still need them to function. Without that protection, I'm afraid greed would cause them to be litigated into oblivion.

Please, dear reader, do not construe this as a lack of concern for the unspeakable losses suffered by the families of the September 11th victims. I pray for them daily, as I'm sure you do. I want to help them, as I'm sure you do. I just think that help should come out of my charitable pocket and not my tax pocket. My old Aunt Nell used to say that charity begins at home.

I never heard her mention anything about the government getting involved.

Golf Addict Confesses Ease with Affliction

JANUARY 31, 2002 : A golfer by the name of Mark Twain once said, "Golf is a good walk spoiled."Raymond Floyd said that golf is so named because "all the other four-letter words were taken."

They're right, you know. Golf is truly a cursed affliction.

I feel I'm qualified to conduct this discourse because, of course, I'm often found on the course these days. You see, I, too, am a golfaholic.

My mama didn't raise me to be a golfer. In fact, she steered me away from such dissipations as John Barleycorn, devil nicotine and idle pastimes like billiards and "cow pasture pool" as it was known in Marfa, Texas, where I was first imprinted with life's truisms.

Out there in west Texas, folks just didn't believe in wasting a perfectly good day chasing a stupid, little white ball around when you could be doing something useful, like roping or feeding the hogs or hunting arrowheads or swimming in a cow tank.

There weren't even any golf courses around. They had a fellow try to construct one out of some pasture land one time, but he canceled the project after the townsfolk got together and convinced him that a golf course would be the laughingstock of all the ranchers in the area, and that he could make more money by not growing something on his pasture. Back then, The Government paid you more to not grow something than you could make by growing something.

Anyway, it wasn't until I moved to Wichita that I succumbed to the siren song of the temptress golf. I took it up under the guise of playing with customers and my sons, who were beginning to play by that time. My mom was shocked when she found out and, I'm sure, was convinced that her oldest boy had lost his direction.

The necessity of earning a living kept me off the course through the week, but as time passed I found my Saturdays and Sundays gradually giving in to the lure of the links. I fell in with bad companions who were also afflicted.

It wasn't long before my weekends were consumed by this ever-encroaching addiction. Whenever I went in to a pro shop, boom! There went the egg money. I tried every club, every new ball, every new gimmick that the evil purveyors of this dastardly pastime propagated, believing each time that I would surely lower my handicap from the triple digits.

I practiced until my hands bore calluses. Every round, no matter how disastrous, would produce enough "be back" shots to ensure that this poor fallen soul would indeed be back to try again for the golden chalice of a par round.

As time passed, my handicap did come down some and rests now at a respectable 16, which is low enough to get me into games with the big boys, who delight in stripping my hard-earned dollars from me without mercy.

I have, at long last, come to terms with the fact that I am forever condemned to pursue the unattainable prize. I will for the remainder of my life be found prowling the fairways, fixing divots and stalking the greens in search of a satisfactory round. The thing that so drained my youth, sapped my strength and depleted my financial resources remains embedded in me like an unquenchable thirst or an unscratchable itch.

I am doomed to seek the company of other sadistic and questionable characters who suffer from the same affliction, for they bring me solace in the knowledge that there are others as wretched as I. We weekend warriors wander down the cart path of life, bound together by a shared obsession, drooling over the skills of Tiger, Duval and their ilk, convinced that the golf god will surely soon favor us with yet another "be back" shot.

Oh, grieve not for me, dear reader, but know that I am content in my misery. Know that the clouds of desolation are quickly parted for me when the sun is shining, the birds are singing, and the lush, green fairways stretch out before me, inviting conquest.

Know that I am most comforted by the click of the club as it advances the ball, the ping of the putter as it seeks the cup, and the howls of obscenities from the devious despots that form my foursome as the putt glides in.

Dang, I so love the smell of a new package of Titleists in the morning!

Lonely Heart Waits for a Loving Home

February 21, 2002 : He's in a cage. He peers out nervously from behind the steel bars. He hears the clanking of other steel doors all around him, and each loud clatter startles him and causes him to tremble. The others like him whine and moan and shout their fears and confusion to an unhearing silence. Occasionally, when he can stand it no longer, he, too, cries out in despair and loneliness.

How long has he been here? He has no sense of the time elapsed. It seems as if all he held dear has faded into a dark, foggy yesterday, and it's harder and harder to remember the faces of those he loved. Where did they go? How did he get separated from them? Did he anger them? Is he being punished for transgressions he can't remember?

No. It was the storm. The awful, crashing, thundering storm that came upon them from out of nowhere. He ran to get away from the terrible noise and lightning. He ran till he could no longer hear the roar, that terrible roar. When at last it subsided, he lay down in a dark place, out of breath, his heart pounding in panic and exhaustion. He tried to stay awake in case the storm resumed, but merciful sleep rolled over him like a tide.

He does not know how long he slept, only that the warm sun and a car honking in the distance awoke him. The air smelled sweet and moist, a leftover from the night before. He became aware of a gnawing hunger, and it instantly reminded him of home. He must go home. He stood and looked around. Panic set in again as he realized that he had no idea where he was. How far had he run last night? Where was he?

He wandered the streets for days, dodging cars, foraging for food where he could find it, avoiding the strangers who called to him. He was searching for home and fighting the growing fear that he'd never find it.

Finally, ragged, worn, dirty and hurting with hunger, he crawled into the lady's car. Maybe she knew where home was. She took him to her house, bathed him and fed him the best meal he'd had in days. She talked gently and lovingly to him, stroked him and made him feel warm, like he used to feel when he was home. She explained to him that he couldn't stay and brought him to this place.

He watched her drive away, thinking that it would have been nice to stay with her in the event he couldn't find home. The people here were nice, too. They talked to him and fed him and even had a doctor check him over. Must be some kind of hospital where they bring those who've been homeless; others like him were coming and going. The place was big and had many rooms. It wasn't as nice as home, and he didn't particularly like the concrete cage he slept in, but it was better than the streets.

All hope of returning home has gone now. He knows he had a home once, but he can't remember the faces of the people who lived there with him, only the warmth that he felt when he was there. He now dwells on the hope that someone else will like him enough to take him to their home and let him live there. Someone like the nice lady who brought him here.

People come in every day and walk down the row of cages, looking in. When they come by, he looks as eager as he can, and wags his tail as his expression silently pleads, "Take ME home with you!"

They stop and smile and let him lick their fingers, then go on.

He lies down, nose between his paws, eyes ever watchful, and waits. Maybe tomorrow someone will want him. Surely tomorrow, someone will come.

And so he waits.

For more information on adopting a loving pet, please contact your local humane society or animal rescue foundation.

Some Things Just Get Mike's Nanny Goat

FEBRUARY 28, 2002 : My grandmother had a saying that has stuck with me all these years. Whenever I got mad, she'd say, "What's the matter? Did something get your nanny goat?"

In grandmother-ese, that means "Did something get under your skin?" or "Is something bothering you?" I've never forgotten that saying, and it's a common phrase in our family's vocabulary and a constant reminder of my grandmother's knack for good old, down-to-earth Texas sayings.

What brought it to mind is thinking about stuff that bugs me these days. These are dumb little things for the most part, but they do get my nanny goat, and since you're reading and I'm writing, I feel the urge to unburden myself to you. Here are some things that get my nanny goat:

— People who use their car horns like a telegraph machine.

In traffic the other day I happened to get in front of a guy who didn't like the way I drove and communicated his dislike by sending Morse code with his danged horn. Beep-beep, beep-beep-beep, beeeep! I finally pulled over and let him roar by, and for a moment I wished I could hit him upside the head with a wet skunk. (Honk at this, you horn-happy bubble brain!) Suffice it to say that for one brief moment, I, Mr. Cool, experienced industrial-strength road rage. I calmed down and continued on, but that guy truly got my nanny goat!

— Corporations that buy successful local businesses, then proceed to make them unsuccessful.

These outfits pay perfectly good money for a successful company and then proceed to dismantle it in the name of consolidation. They first announce that they plan no changes, and then they begin the changes. They lay people off, drive away customers with abrupt policy changes, and withdraw community support in an effort to pad a shrinking bottom line. You have to wonder why they bought the business in the first place if it needed so many changes.

We've seen a bunch of these takeovers in Wichita in the past several years, and although there are exceptions, I think we're worse for the wear. The smart ones (unfortunately, there aren't many smart corporations) recognize that community relationships are valuable assets and that community support is also very good business. The stupid ones (unfortunately, there are many stupid corporations) continue to downsize and consolidate until the business they purchased is decimated. In their wake they leave disrupted lives and broken careers. Yep. That gets my nanny goat!

— Remote controls that don't work.

There's nothing more frustrating than sitting in front of a TV set, clicking away with no response. For a man, this is the ultimate feeling of powerlessness. I threw a remote control into the creek the other day after clicking away for an hour with no response. As I watched it sail into the air,

I remembered that I hadn't changed the batteries for a while. That got my nanny goat!

— Waiting on the phone for an hour, listening to elevator music, while some deep-voiced doofus keeps reminding me that my call is important to them.

If my call was so danged important to them, they wouldn't make me wait for an hour. I know I've griped about automated phone service before, but it seems to be getting worse.

I'll bet we'd be shocked if we knew how many man-hours were tied up in waiting to talk to a real, live person. My suspicion is that the main perpetrators of this time-waster are corporations that buy up the local businesses and convert to automated systems in the name of efficiency. Never mind the fact that it inconveniences the heck out of customers. That really gets my nanny goat!

There are, of course, other things that get my nanny goat, but these are the tops of my list, and since I've unloaded them sufficiently, I'll stop my bleating for now.

Besides, I have to go buy a new remote control.

Sales People Make the World Go Around

MARCH 7, 2002 : Sales is a noble profession. It's much maligned as a profession, but it is indeed noble. I didn't always know that. I used to think that selling was a terrible job, and that all salespeople were high-pressure con artists.

When I was a kid selling Los Angeles Examiners door to door to earn milkshake money, I learned that most people don't really like salespeople much. I had a lot of doors slammed in my face, but I did earn enough to keep me in milkshakes! I learned that rejection is a way of life for a salesperson, and I didn't like it much.

It wasn't until years later that I developed a whole new attitude about the profession of selling, and learned that salespeople are the lifeblood of any business and, in fact, of the economy itself.

Consider the fact that nothing much happens in a business until somebody sells something. A manufacturer can produce products all day long, but unless someone sells those products to customers, the manufacturer will soon be out of business.

I can't think of a single product or service that doesn't need a salesperson to market it to customers. With a good sales force, a business will prosper; without good salesmanship, a business is doomed to failure.

Yet, interestingly, the profession is not highly regarded. Not long ago I saw a poll taken among college students that ranked professions, and sales was dead last. Not surprising considering the Willy Loman and Herb Tarlek images conjured up by the media, which portray the salesman as a fast-talking, loud-dressing hotshot with a streak of carny in his pitch.

While I'm sure that such a character exists in the profession, I doubt that he's very successful. Today's successful salesperson is a professional who doesn't "pitch" customers but rather helps them buy the product.

Today's successful salesperson, by the way, lives very well. Most work on a commission as opposed to a salary, and the more they sell, the more they make. A good salesperson never has to ask for a raise and never has to worry about a job.

Companies are eager to hire and retain good salespeople, and the smart ones listen to their salespeople's input when it comes to company policy.

I didn't say that it's easy to be a salesperson. The profession requires hard work, organizational skills, high energy and empathy (for one's customers), knowledge and a healthy enough ego to shake off the rejection that is inevitable. A good salesperson must be a good listener, and above all else focused on the customers needs. To the extent that he or she detects those needs and fills them, the salesperson will be successful.

You might say that the plus side of a sales career, if you are good at it, is high earnings, freedom and the satisfaction of serving others. The down side is the rejection, the fact that your income is totally dependent on your next sale, and the need to be constantly on call to your customers. There is no greater feeling than closing a sale, and no worse feeling than losing one. Both come with the territory.

So here's to the salespeople of the world. Here's to those guys and gals who sell the cars, the clothes, the insurance, the advertising, the groceries, the toothpaste, the newspapers, the pizza, the securities, and all the rest of the stuff we buy. Here's to you for the contribution you make to a thriving economy and the way of life we've grown accustomed to.

The next time a door is slammed in your face or a cranky customer is rude to you, or you wake up on a cold morning without a clue about where your next sale is coming from, know that you do participate in a noble profession. Know that you are noble also in your fortitude and perseverance. Know that you are the lifeblood of our economic system!

I learned to appreciate sales as a profession when it dawned on me that everybody is in sales. We are all selling an idea, a belief, a concept, an attitude or a set of values.

We are all salespeople.

Power Is Not in the Hands of Everyone

MARCH 21, 2002 : A few years ago, one of those business gurus introduced the word empowerment to the corporate world.

In that context, the word meant giving employees and customers the power to control the way they interacted with the business and its products and services. The term ranked up there with other pop-culture buzz words like corporate culture, team and quality circles. It implied that the employee or customer had power.

Since power is a basic condition that appeals to most of us, the term is still pretty popular. However, one only has to examine the events of the past couple of years to see that employees and customers have not really been empowered to do anything.

Ask any employee who has been downsized or any customer who has been put on hold for two hours if they feel empowered. Ask an Enron employee if he or she feels powerful. No, sir, power is all around us, but it ain't necessarily in the hands of the ordinary folk.

I was thinking the other day about who actually does have power, though, and came up with this list:

— Politicians. They have a heck of a deal. They get to collect money from us and buy stuff they want us to have - and in fairness, stuff we want to have, such as roads and bridges. Having control over our money makes for megapower for these folks because they get to make the laws that govern how much of our money is collected and how much of it they spend. On occasion, they even give us back a piddling of our money in the form of tax refunds and grants and various programs, as long as we do what they say. That, brother, is power!

— Lawyers. They have power because they go to school and learn how to interpret the gazillion laws that those dang politicians make up. We ordinary mortals can't begin to comprehend the complexity of all these laws, so we have to hire lawyers who can. Since most politicians were lawyers at one time, they have the power to make laws that only their own kind can figure out. In today's world, if you are a lawyer, you have power.

— Tax accountants. These folks are powerful because they are the only ones who can figure out the darn tax codes. The tax laws are so complicated that you need a tax accountant just to pay your taxes or get one of those refunds. Let's face it: If your tax guy says you owe money, you pay it! We usually don't even question him or her, because there isn't a snowball's chance in the hot place that we'd have a clue about how much we owe, or are owed. That, too, is power.

— Doctors. They have power because they get to tell us when we're sick, what we should do about it, when we should do it, and how much it's going to cost. Doctors can hold our lives in their hands every day. For sheer, unadulterated power, no one tops a doctor.

— Teachers. They have the power to shape our children's minds and personalities. This is a great power indeed. Teachers' power can ultimately determine the progress of our world by the ideas and attitudes they implant in our children. Just for the record, these folks are underpaid, but make no mistake about it. They are powerful!

— Media. They are powerful because most of us are too busy or too lazy to think for ourselves, so the media get to do it for us. This gives those in the media sway over what we think and talk about. That, too, is raw power.

— Alan Greenspan. I put him on my list because he has the power to crater the stock market by raising his left eyebrow and send it soaring by just wiggling his nose. I also believe that he's powerful because he has learned to speak a language that no one else can understand, and hence power accrues to him because his pronouncements are so unin-telligible that they seem profound. Any way you slice it, he's a powerful dude.

We could regain some of the power that we've delegated by getting to know the candidates we vote for, by paying more attention to the laws they make, by taking better care of ourselves, by demanding higher media standards and by spending more time instructing our own children. We don't do this much anymore because our lives have become too busy and we are too preoccupied.

So we have delegated to others the responsibility for collecting and spending our tax money, interpreting our laws, curing our ills, deciding our agenda and teaching our children.

Talk about empowerment!

Reflections, Forecasts of the Seasons of Our Lives

APRIL 4, 2002 : It occurred to me the other day that the poets and writers who have compared our lives to the seasons of the year were pretty darned wise.

These momentous mind meanderings came on the heels of a good report from my doctor. If you consider that a person's life has four distinct seasons, it all starts to make sense. Though it's been done far more eloquently, here's my take on the similarities.

The spring of our lives occurs from birth to about 20 years of age. It's when everything is new and fresh. In the early days of this spring we learn to communicate our basic needs. We learn to taste, to feel, to care and to want. Like the trees and flowers that bud and show themselves in the first warm days of the season, our personalities begin to emerge.

In this season, life is warm and comfortable. Curiosity abounds as we sense for the first time the many pleasures of discovery. For most of us, it's a bright, happy time when problems are few, and the days roll by fueled with boundless energy and exuberance. In the freshness of this season, all things seem possible and time is expendable, as we believe we have an endless supply.

It is this season that I will remember and long for the rest of my life. In my spring, I fell in love for the first time, found my life's calling and began my journey toward a rich and fulfilling career in a business that I loved.

The summer of our lives begins at about 20 and lasts until about 50. This season brings responsibilities and challenges and produces many opportunities for accomplishment.

This is the season of striving in the sun, reaching for the stars and daring the unthinkable. It's the time when failure cannot deter us and success only brings the thirst for more success. In the summer of our lives we are impassioned, opinionated and driven. We make mistakes during this time that we tend to shrug off as we push forward, propelled by ambition and the desire to achieve, to acquire wealth and material things. We race through this season without thought to the depletion of our allotted days and weeks.

I can truthfully say now that my summer was almost a blur. Thirty years passed in the blink of an eye. I married, we had children, they grew to adults and moved away, our business grew and prospered, and it all transpired in what now seems like a nanosecond to me. Sometimes I'm amazed at how fast the days of my summer flew by and startled by the awareness that they are irretrievable.

The autumn of our lives begins at about 50 and lasts until about 75. The pace becomes less hectic, the beat becomes less intense, and we begin to enjoy the quality of life that we strove so vigorously for in our summer.

Our values change, and we cherish friends more as their headstones become more plentiful along the way. In this season the material goals once so necessary to happiness seem somehow less important, when achieved, than the nearness of our loved ones and the presence of good health.

Maladies begin to creep into our lives as

our bodies, like overripe fruit, begin to deteriorate and weaken. Like trees shedding leaves in the fall, we begin to downsize, to simplify and prepare for the oncoming winter.

I woke up one morning in the middle of my autumn and found myself saddened by loss, fearful of illness and suddenly cognizant of the fact that the days of my seasons are dwindling. On that morning I resolved to make the most of my remaining days of autumn, to do all that I could to restore my health and to seek solace in the arms of those who care for me, so that the decade of my autumn that I hope remains will provide good memories.

It is these memories, you see, that will be the logs for the fire I stoke in the winter of my life. If I make it to that winter, I know its chill could indeed be bleak and cold, for it is our final season. It is the season in which we return to the earth, frail, aged and infirm.

I dread the winter; I long for the spring and summer of my yesterday, and revel in the golden days of autumn that yet await me.

Rude Folks Reflect Their Poor Upbringing

APRIL 18, 2002 : Whew! For a while there I figured I was the only one who thought the world was getting ruder.

I thought I was just becoming what we used to call an old fogy about the fact that my fellow Americans seem, as a whole, to be less considerate of folks around them. I've actually heard myself mumbling, "In my day people were not so rude." (A sure sign that I must be tottering over into senility.)

Now it appears that I'm not the only person who senses the rudening of America. A recent Public Agenda research group survey of 2,013 people across the country found that 88 percent said they had sometimes come across people who were rude or disrespectful; 79 percent said that lack of respect and courtesy is a serious problem; 62 percent allowed as how it bothers them a lot when they see rude and disrespectful behavior in public; 41 percent even admitted to occasionally being guilty of rude behavior themselves.

Over half of those interviewed said they had walked out of a store in the past year because of poor customer service; half said they often have to put up with other folks talking on cellular phones in a loud and annoying manner; and six in 10 said they regularly observe others driving aggressively or recklessly.

Ha! See there? I'm NOT an old fogy! If I am, there are at least 2,013 other old fogies like me out there! If this survey's findings are accurate, why is rudeness an apparently increasing fact of life? The focus groups conducted by the Public Agenda research folks seemed to suggest that this epidemic is occurring because of overcrowding in malls and stadiums and other public places, or that perhaps it's caused by the ever-increasing pace of our lives in general.

I don't believe any of that baloney. I think rudeness is on the rise due to one simple fact: People are rude. They're rude because they weren't taught any better. They weren't taught any better because their parents were rude. Rude parents make rude children.

Polite people (there are still some around) got that way because they were taught good manners. Boys were taught that it's not nice to swear in front of ladies and children. Kids had to pass a courtesy test before they were allowed to drive. Children were taught to say *yes, ma'am* or *yes, sir,* and *please* and *thank you.* Those lessons, once learned, are habits that stay with you all your life. Unfortunately, the absence of those habits also stays with a person for life.

I'm sure there are people who just do not know they are rude and disrespectful because they weren't taught to know the difference. I feel kind of sorry for those folks and wonder whether maybe they would change if confronted with their condition. I also suspect there are those who know darn well that they are rude and disrespectful and like it that way. I doubt they'll ever change, and the condition will likely be passed on to their offspring.

The best way to keep from responding to rudeness with rudeness (the condition can be infectious) is to avoid these clowns. You can avoid them by watching for them and not crossing their paths. They're often seen screaming into a cell phone, or flipping you the finger as they zoom around you in traffic, or berating the ticket people at the airport or sprinkling their conversation with as many four-letter words as they can muster, or lighting up a cigar or cigarette and blowing the smoke in your face.

Instead of being fogy-ish and continually griping about these inconsiderate folks, I thought about having little mini-interventions with each one as I encounter them. I would, I figured, take them aside, look them squarely in the eye and say, "You know, YOU are just plain RUDE!"

I decided not to do that, though.

It would be too rude.

Health, Friends and Memory Are Temporary

APRIL 25, 2002 : Taking certain things for granted, I suppose, is a human trait. We sail along for the duration of our time here on earth, claiming sovereignty over life's conditions as if we were feudal lords, entitled by the simple act of being born.

As we grow long of tooth, it becomes abundantly clear that in reality there is precious little that we can take for granted. We learn that we are not so anointed after all. We learn that life is a constant evolution, producing constant change and chaos, and that there are no perpetual grants, only temporary ones.

I know all of this to be factual by my own experiences these past two or three years. Stubbornly and reluctantly, I've come to realize that many things I've taken for granted for most of my adult life ain't necessarily so.

Take memory, for instance. There was a time when I'd stand my memory of events, facts, names and details up to anyone's. I could speak with certainty, knowing that I was as right as rain and that my recollections were dead accurate.

Now, I find myself less and less sure that my memory is intact. I have to put my brain in search mode sometimes just to remember an acquaintance's first name. I'm constantly surprised when some longtime friend will speak of an instance in our past of which I have no recollection.

I used to be able to identify thousands of songs after hearing the first three bars. Now sometimes the whole song comes and goes and I'm still trying to identify the art-

ist, whose name resides right on the tip of my tongue but maddeningly out of reach.

I have recently started writing intended tasks down, lest they slip off my radar screen, and have consigned all appointment setting to my secretary, lest I space out on future commitments.

I saw an ad the other day for some herbal stuff that would improve memory and thought about taking it, but I forgot the name of it! Suffice it to say that I no longer take memory for granted.

I used to take physical fitness for granted. I could bounce up and hit the floor with vigor and never slow down the whole day. Nowadays, a little sit-down is a welcome event. Trouble is, after sitting for a while, the simple act of getting up becomes a tester. I creak! Muscles I didn't know I had attack me, and limbs go to sleep on me.

I fancy that just getting out of a chair and walking the first few steps makes me look like the late Walter Brennan hobbling down the street. Anyway, I no longer take fitness for granted.

I used to take hair for granted. Now I know, after my bout with chemo, that hair can be given and hair can be taken away. I can't tell you how exhilarating it is now to have to go to the barber again, or to have someone say, "Your hair is messed up." No, sir. I will NEVER take hair for granted again!

I took eyesight for granted for years. I've worn glasses for distance forever, but it always stuns me when the optometrist kicks up the prescription because I can't read those dang little letters even with my last pair of glasses on. While I'm still not convinced that they don't just shrink those letters a little each year, I'm not taking eyesight for granted these days.

I took my friends for granted for years also. I always assumed that there would be ample time to spend with them down the road, and all too often I put off telling them of their value to my well-being by rationalizing how busy I was. The increasing number of funerals I've attended in recent years has awakened me to the need to never again take friendship for granted.

I took good health for granted. Boy, did I! The only time I was in a hospital was to visit. Now I know that good health is not an entitlement but a precious privilege. I realize at long last that for most of us, good health is a temporary grant to be cherished and maintained by constant attention to healthy eating and exercise and abstinence from harmful substances.

The departure and subsequent return of good health has forever cured this ol' boy of ever taking it for granted again.

In fact, the ONLY thing I'm taking for granted these days is that you can't take anything for granted.

CHUCK & MARGE KING   BILL & DEBBIE LUCAS   MIKE & PEGI OATMAN   MONT & GEORGIA DRAPER

Recalling the Sweet Music of Childhood

MAY 9, 2002 : I used to think that Mother's Day was a secret plot by the florists of America to make all of us errant, wayward sons feel guilty so we'd order up the most extravagant bouquets we could afford and frantically speed them on their way to our long-neglected mothers.

These days, I know better.

Mother's Day is truly a blessing. If your Mom is still alive, it prods you to make the contact that means so much to her and, ultimately, to you. If, like my Mom, she has passed on to a better place, it bids you to pause and recollect with tenderness the affection of one who loved you more than any other.

My Mom was one of the most talented women I've ever met. She was a concert pianist who delighted the folks in Marfa, Texas, with her recitals when she was as young as 15. She played the violin beautifully, and I can shut my eyes, even today, and hear her playing *Ave Maria* on the violin or Beethoven on the grand piano in the living room of my grandparents' house, where we lived for a time.

In another place or time, there's no doubt that Mom would have been a featured player in a symphony orchestra in some big city. She was that good. She was widowed twice before she was 30, and her music buoyed her, I'm sure, through some mighty lean times. A year before he died, my stepfather gave me her violin, which is more than 100 years old. While I can't play a lick on it, sometimes when I take it down and hold it I can hear her playing her wonderfully sweet melodies.

MARY OATMAN

She was also a gifted artist. She worked in oils and watercolors, and when she wasn't wiping our noses and cooking dinner, she could be found painting the west Texas landscapes and vistas of New Mexico and Arizona that surrounded us as we moved about, following my stepdad's construction work.

She was often commissioned to paint for patrons who discovered her ability, but she mostly painted for herself and for her family. My brother and sisters and I and several of our relatives have walls adorned with her canvases and handmade frames. They are striking in their exquisite perfection, and in the way they reveal her talent for seeing and replicating the beauty of the Southwest. She never said much about her painting ability, and I often wonder if she knew just how good she was.

Mom was also a wonderful seamstress. She sewed her own clothes, made clothes for us kids all through grade school, and could quilt with the best of them. One of my earliest Christmas memories is a stick horse she made for me out of an old sock and a sawed-off broomstick, with buttons for eyes. She made our Halloween costumes every year, and they were always better than the other kids' store-bought stuff.

When I started a country dance band in high school, Mom made our outfits, and they rivaled Porter Wagoner's for fanciness. I spoke with one of those musicians the other day, and he told me he still has two of those getups, yet 40 years later.

Mom closed her eyes for the last time in a hospital room in El Paso a few years ago. She was surrounded by all of her children, her grandchildren, daughters- and sons-in-law and her third and last husband of more than 40 years.

In the hours before she lost consciousness, she joked about how she had to get sick to get us all together, once again reminding us of her marvelous sense of humor. A little after 4 in the afternoon, she opened her eyes and said, "I see a river," let out a deep sigh and slipped away. Then the strangest thing happened. It was as if we could feel her spirit hovering over us for a few minutes, and then it, too, was gone. We've spoken of it several times since then, and all of us felt that same sensation at precisely the same moment.

Many times I've caught myself thinking I should call my mother or send her a note, only to be rudely reminded that I cannot. As this Mother's Day approaches, I find myself wishing I'd done better in that department.

For many, Sunday will mean buying and sending flowers and cards. For me, it will mean taking down an old, dusty violin and hearing an echo from my childhood. The echo of a beautiful and talented young mother playing *Ave Maria* as sweetly as it's ever been played.

The Real Treasures in Life Are Found with the Heart

MAY 23, 2002 : Here's a premise for you. In life, it's not what you know, or even who you know that is significant.

It's what you feel.

That's right. What you feel is more important than what you know. I offer this premise up for your consideration as one who did not always understand it.

Like many, I spent years as a bonafide, living, breathing, note-taking, phone-talking, schedule-keeping workaholic. I worked 13-hour days and scoffed at those who didn't do the same. I routinely planned my family time subject to my work time. Work came first, and everything else came second.

I was, in short, driven. Driven to succeed. Driven to accomplish. Driven to take care of business as a struggling radio station co-owner. I broke each part of my day into quarter-hour segments and filled each one with something productive. I did that for nearly 40 years.

Along the way my wife and I raised three kids (though she did most of the raising), traveled some and had but a few friends outside my business circles.

The pace I lived propelled me through those years at a breakneck speed, blurring the events and personalities that I encountered into a giant decoupage of faces, awards, problems, accomplishments, purchases and performances. It now seems that it all happened in only the blink of an eye, yet it was the best part of four decades, the majority of my life!

It's funny how a journey seems endless when you embark, and seems only a nanosecond long in retrospect after you have arrived. Since my journey is ongoing, I can't say that I've arrived, only that I've paused at a mile marker to catch a breath and reflect. As I've reflected, it has dawned on me that what you feel is what you remember. For instance, I can't remember my first successful business deal. But I can see as clearly as if it were yesterday Mike Lynch's big hand extended for a shake that sealed our 40-year partnership.

I can't remember my first sale, but I can remember the dimples in my daughter Melissa's cheeks as I stared at her for the first time through the hospital nursery window and realized that she was my firstborn.

I can't remember all the details about the people I hired over the years, but I can remember the enormous sense of pride I felt the first time I realized that my oldest son, Andy, was going to follow me into my chosen profession.

I can't remember when our station first became No. 1 in the market, but I still get a lump in my throat when I remember my youngest son, Richard, giving me the thumbs-up sign in the rearview mirror as he steered his car onto the freeway and away to college. I can't remember the little problems that plagued our business from week to week, but I can remember the tears we shed as we buried our old dog, Traveler, out in the front yard in the pouring rain after 15 years of faithful companionship.

I can't recall what song was No. 1 on

our radio station in any given week, but I can remember the silence in the room as my mother slipped away after a long and horrendous bout with cancer, and I can still feel the gratitude we all felt for her peace so fitfully won.

I can't remember the details of the many acquisitions we made during our business life, but I can recollect with great clarity the good friends who have come into my life over those years.

Would I still be a certified workaholic, knowing what I know now? Probably. But I'd like to think that I'd be wiser, perhaps kinder and more aware of the importance of emotions.

I'd care more about feelings and less about facts. I'd listen to my heart more and my head less, and I think I'd collect more of those special, golden, emotional moments that turn into memories, and be less concerned about the minutia that flit by like so many thistles in the wind.

It turns out, you see, that those moments are the real treasures of life, for they are life itself.

All the rest of it is just background noise.

The World Would Be Better Off without Ties

MAY 30, 2002 : I have a modest proposal that I think will go a long way toward making the world a better place in which to live. The idea came to me not long ago when I was getting ready to go to a rather formal dinner that called for business attire, which as you know means a suit and one of those danged neckties.

Now mind you, I'm not a stranger to neckties. I wore them most every day for 40 years until I retired a couple of years ago, and in fact, I still have most of the ties I ever owned hanging in my closet. (You never throw them away, 'cause soon as you do, they come back into style.)

The plain fact of the matter is neckties are about the most useless things ever invented. I mean, most other articles of men's clothing have a practical purpose: keeping a fellow warm, covering up stuff that should be covered up, hiding a gut or broadening shoulders. Neckties, as far as I can see, serve no useful purpose except to choke a man into submission, humbling him when he goes out into the world to ply his trade or to take the little woman to that dinner party that requires business attire.

Just learning to tie one of the cursed things is a humbling experience. My wife used to think I had Tourette's syndrome in the morning as I stood in front of a mirror trying to get the knot right or the length properly adjusted. She finally got to the point where the kids had to be outside in the yard playing before Dad could turn the air blue while knotting his tie.

Besides being hard to tie, the dad-gummed things just look stupid. I mean, if you wear a colorful, flowery one, it looks like Walt Disney's worst nightmare. If you wear a plain red one, it looks like a lizard tongue hanging down from your Adam's apple. If you don't pull it up tight, the knot hangs down and looks sloppy; if you do pull it up tight, you can't swallow your food 'cause you're choking.

Most all the ties I have are decorated with remnants of the meal I ate the last time I wore them. That's because ties are always flopping down into your mashed potatoes or sloshing around in your corn chowder.

Tie manufacturers are pretty clever. They obviously got together at some big necktie summit and figured out how to control planned obsolescence. The minute you buy a wide tie, narrow ties become fashionable. The day after you buy a half dozen narrow ones, wide ones are back! No, sir, I think it's time that we men just say no to ties.

That's my idea, see. I figure that if all of us men simply quit wearing those darned things, we can change the world. Think of it. You could wear golf shirts, or T-shirts, or sport shirts to those fancy affairs.

Look at the benefits: Men would be in a better mood because they wouldn't have to wrestle with tying one of the dumb things; they'd be far more comfortable at work and hence more productive; the wife would benefit by her man being much more willing to go out to those dinners and affairs that call for business attire.

If you doubt the wisdom of my modest proposal, walk into any bank that has gone to casual Fridays. The loan officers are actually smiling, and everyone seems happy and pleasant, as opposed to the severe, scrunched-up frowns you see through the week when bankers are required to look like Brooks Brothers fashion ads.

Who knows? Future generations may learn that ties were the cause of male-pattern baldness or the dreaded paunch that men seem to develop after years of having their blood flow cut off at the neck. Heck, look at the folks in Hawaii. They don't wear ties and they're always smiling and wearing leis and playing the ukulele. Men, we could be like that!

What would it hurt if we all just declared a one-year moratorium on ties? I predict that if we did, we'd never go back to them. And when your grandchildren want to know what you accomplished in life, you could say with pride that your generation threw off the ties that bind and forever changed the definition of business attire.

Are you with me?

I Wish I Had Said All This to My Father

JUNE 13, 2002 : My natural father died in a trucking accident before my brother, and I ever knew him. A couple of years after his death, Mom married again. Before long my sister was born, and Mom kissed her second husband goodbye as he went to serve in the Air Force during World War II.

I was too young to have but the vaguest recollection of him, but I have strong memories of my mother lying across the bed crying, clutching the telegram informing her of his death in a plane crash. I think I was five years old at the time. Mom worked to support us, and we lived with my grandparents in our old Marfa homestead until she met Goatie.

His real name was Arthur, but around town he was Goatie. They were married in 1948, and we became a family. Along the way, my uncle's daughter came to live with us when her mother died in childbirth, and Mom and Goatie set about raising four kids. He formally adopted all of us a couple of years later, and our name became Oatman.

Goatie and all of us grew up in west Texas, where people are pretty stoic about life and don't easily express their feelings. I guess that's why we always called him by his nickname and never referred to him as Dad or Father. He was good to us, but we never talked much. Mom did all of the fussing and disciplining necessary to raise four kids, and Goatie made the living.

In what now seems like the blink of an eye, we all grew up, got married and moved away. Mom passed away in 1996, and Goatie grieved after her until his death three years later.

ARTHUR "GOATIE" OATMAN

I've been thinking about him a lot as Father's Day approaches, and it occurs to me that I wish I'd said a lot of things to him that I never did say.

A lot of what I know today, I learned from him. Although he never lectured, he taught. He showed me how to whittle, how to open a pecan with a pocket knife, how to drive nails straight and how to handle a saw. He showed me how to drive a bulldozer and how to handle a shovel. I never even knew he was teaching me things, so unobtrusive was his gentle instruction, but he showed me lots of stuff that I still know how to do today.

I wish I'd told him that.

I appreciated his pride in me. He never directly told me, but I could tell he was proud when I'd overhear him repeating stories to his friends about things I'd done. He'd usually chuckle and tell on me, but never in a demeaning way, always with pride.

I wish I'd told him that.

Even though he never raised a hand to me in all the years we lived with him, his approval if I deserved it or his disapproval if I deserved that was the discipline that guided me down a fairly straight and narrow path. I wasn't perfect by a long shot, but I always gauged my actions by what I thought he'd think if he found out.

I wish I'd told him that.

I was aware of the sacrifices he made to provide for his adopted family. He worked for wages that today are way below the poverty line to put a roof over our heads and food on our table. And when the times got tough he was resilient and talented enough to handle a variety of jobs: carpenter, truck driver, heavy-equipment operator, construction foreman.

He did them all and never complained about the early mornings, long days, hard work, or low pay - least I never heard him complain. Whenever I thought I had it rough in my career, all I had to do was remember that he worked twice as hard for a tenth of the wages, and I could go on.

I wish I'd told him that.

I wish I'd told Dad that even though he wasn't my natural father, he was my real father. He took us in and raised us like we were his own, and in every way he was a father, the only one I and my brother and sisters ever knew.

I wish I'd told him that.

Late in Life Dad Learns Lesson in Fatherhood

JUNE 27, 2002 : I had a great talk with my son the other day. We were sitting outside, under the trees on the deck, watching his youngest swim in the old backyard pool just as my son had done years before. He'd come up to visit for Father's Day, and the time was ripe for a good old-fashioned visit.

During the conversation he allowed as how he often resented some of the encounters he and I experienced when he was growing up. He was talking, of course, about the times he'd gotten into trouble by stepping over the rather strict lines I had drawn as a dad trying to raise perfect children, and more specifically about my reaction to those infractions.

He confessed that for years he'd felt that I had punished him unfairly and harshly. He recounted four or five incidents, most of which I didn't remember, and told how they had caused him to harbor an apparently deep-seated resentment of his dad. Only recently, he said, had he begun to realize that there were many other things he could focus on that were much more pleasant and made those "injustices" seem insignificant.

He said that being a parent had taught him that sometimes, out of love and concern for the child's well-being, parents make mistakes. I confessed to him that I knew I had made many mistakes as a father, mostly on the side of strictness, and would do many things differently if I could do them over.

After he left, I got to thinking about what some of those things might be.

The most significant thing, I believe, is

that I would treat each child as an individual. In those days I had a tendency to hand out the rules and punishment without regard for the child's unique reaction.

It wasn't until later in my business, when dealing with employees, that I learned the art of modifying my reactions to fit the individual's personality. People require individual attention. Kids do, too!

I'd give anything if I'd learned that in time to have applied it to my own family. My son, you see, was much more sensitive than his brother and sister, and his dad's disapproval affected him much more deeply than it did his siblings. In his case, a little bit went a long way.

I'd also like to think that I would be more aware of the impact parents have on their children. In children's formative years, we can do no wrong in their eyes. They revere us and crave our love and attention.

We must be very careful not to create the aura of infallibility, for when a child finally realizes that the person he or she admires the most is imperfect, it can be traumatic. My son admitted that when it dawned on him that his old man was human and made mistakes, it confused and bewildered him and added to the resentment he felt. I'd be more careful, if there were a next time, to make sure that he knew that I knew that none of us is perfect, least of all his father.

I guess I'd also try to remember that applies to kids as well. No matter how hard we try or how strict we are, kids will make mistakes. It's how we react to those mistakes that determines how that child will be imprinted by the experience.

Over-react, and the kid will grow to resent you and eventually separate from you, just as an oppressed people will eventually overthrow the government they deem unfair.

Under-react, and the kid grows up undisciplined and with no clear sense of right or wrong. A lack of disciplined structure, I believe, is just as bad as too disciplined a structure.

My lesson late in life has been that one size doesn't fit all. If I were doing it again, I'd tailor the structure and discipline to fit the kid instead of trying to make the kid fit the structure.

As I was reflecting on all of this, I remembered one thing my son said that was neat. "Dad, one thing that I have always appreciated was that you were consistent. I never had to guess what would happen if I stepped over the line. And I knew that no matter what happened, you'd be there to know what to do."

Words of comfort for an old dude who was starting to feel regretful.

I find it amusing now that most of the few parenting skills I have came not from some school or from my own parents, but from my kids. They taught me how to be a parent.

I just wish I'd learned it all when they were young.

Our Own Greed Fueled an Economic Downfall

JULY 11, 2002 : My *Random House College Dictionary* defines the word greedy as "excessively or inordinately desirous of wealth."

It seems to me that we've all become a little too greedy for our own good. Take the stock market, for instance.

Only months ago we were all basking in the sunlight of a roaring bull market and predicting a Dow in excess of 15,000 and a NASDAQ of 7,000. Brokers were touting each new dot-com as the next Microsoft. Mom and Pop were hocking their homes to jump into the market, and the sky was the limit. Formerly prudent investors with balanced portfolios threw caution to the wind and plunged into equities with abandon. We were on a roll, it seemed, and we thought it would last forever.

Well, it didn't. Sagging corporate earnings, the tech fall from grace, and September 11th all did their part to let the wind out of our sails.

Now comes the latest boogieman: corporate dishonesty. Enron and Arthur Andersen, WorldCom, Xerox, Martha Stewart and ImClone, and who the heck knows who's next?

Even in the face of an apparently thriving economy, the investors - big fish and little minnows - are pulling back, licking their wounds and dropping stocks like a bad transmission or a hot horseshoe.

Politicians smell an opportunity, too. The Democrats are blaming the Republicans, and the Republicans are blaming the Democrats, and both are pandering to frustrated investor/voters by proposing new laws and punishment for the newest evildoers: CEOs.

Financial networks hourly are reporting news about the latest scandal and clearly can't wait until they can break the next big one. Stock prices go up and down like yo-yos as rumors whirl around the trading floor like dust devils in west Texas. Retirement savings have been depleted to the point that many retirees are going back to work.

Not a pretty picture, to be sure. The fact is, we had it coming. We all got greedy. We became *inordinately desirous of wealth* and forgot the old adage that what goes up must come down.

The top executives of a few public companies imagined millions of dollars lining their pockets if they could just keep those share prices increasing each quarter. For some, the temptation to cheat was apparently just too great.

We everyday investors were just as *excessively desirous of wealth*, buying those stocks that we thought would make us overnight millionaires without regard for old-fashioned fundamentals like what kind of profit did they earn, how much debt did they have, and how long had they been in business.

We routinely punished companies by tossing their stock into the basement when they failed to promise increasing quarterly earnings, so a few of them began promising good times and cooking the books to make those promises appear to come true.

The financial watchdogs, the accounting folks, apparently were greedy as evidenced by at least one firm's supposed willingness to bend the rules to protect its lucrative accounting and consulting contracts.

I'm like Will Rogers on this subject. All I know is what I read in the papers, but it doesn't take a dad-gummed genius to figure out that greed is what got us into this mess.

I reckon we'll stay in the mess until companies start rewarding their corporate big shots for getting and keeping customers and making good products and providing great service instead of just driving share value. Share value, I think, will follow if they do the other stuff.

I also calculate that investors are going to have to be less punitive toward companies that fail to "meet street expectations" on a quarterly basis and become more interested in the company's long-term success. The Japanese are famous for taking a long-term view and scorning our quarter-to-quarter mentality.

It also may be that we common folks need to adjust our greed-o-meters down a bit, too. We need to remember that the vast majority of America's public companies are good, solid outfits that are investment-worthy and, while maybe not capable of 27 percent increases each quarter, are honestly producing reasonable returns over a reasonable period of time.

I don't know about you, but a little old 6 percent or 7 percent return right now would make me think I'd died and gone to heaven.

Visit with 'Home Folks' Teaches a Life Lesson

JULY 18, 2002 : Sometimes the answers to questions that trouble you are nearer than you think. It was close by in Oklahoma last week that I experienced a kind of resolution that I had been seeking (subconsciously, I suppose) for some time.

You see, I am part of the generation that began moving away from home to succeed. When you move from home, you move from your roots and your kin and sometimes from the values that reside there. You begin a new life that doesn't include the closeness of home folks. You in essence cut the ties that bind you to Mom and Dad and cousins and uncles and aunts and old family friends.

When you're young and on fire with ambition and desire to succeed, it doesn't seem like too much of a sacrifice. You trade the old, familiar faces and customs and surroundings for the new, the busy, the exciting.

Then, slowly but surely, you lose contact with the home folks. Your life takes a different highway than theirs, yours speeding forward through the markets of men, theirs anchored in the bedrock of passed-down beliefs and customs that more and more seem outdated as your new life unfolds. Visits back get fewer and fewer, phone calls home dwindle, and letters are sacrificed to busy schedules.

Then, one day, you are old and reflective, and they are gone. They didn't leave suddenly. They passed on, one by one as age and infirmities claimed their due over time. But to you, their passing seems sudden because you weren't paying attention.

It is only when you are reflective and in search of your past that the enormity of the loss, the absence of their knowledge and the realization that when they died, a part of you did, too, that you begin to comprehend the loss. It becomes an itch that can never be scratched. A longing that forevermore will go unfulfilled, for the home folks are gone.

It was in this state of mind and in this reflective condition that I recently attended the 60th wedding anniversary celebration of Ray and Virginia West in Henryetta, Oklahoma. My wife's aunt and uncle were married in 1942. Now, six decades later, he in his best Sunday-go-to-meeting suit and she in her beautifully flowered dress, adorned with corsages, greeted some 75 uncles, aunts, nieces, nephews, children, grandchildren and church friends.

It was a simple affair, with homemade punch, cookies and pastries from the local bakery, a register for folks to sign and a table with the couple's life on display in family photographs that spanned their 60 years together. It was held at the little church most of them had attended for the better part of their lives, and the room was filled with smiles as big as Oklahoma.

Courtly, snow-topped gentlemen, erect and stoic, gracious and mannerly, teasing "Ol' Ray" with cracks about how lucky he was and how long-suffering she must be to have put up with the likes of him all these years. Pleasant, motherly women chatting, smiling, visiting, all the while helping serve the punch and sherbet and taking turns holding the grandbabies in their arms.

Hugs were everywhere as friends reminisced and relatives caught up on each other's lives and wondered about others they had known. It occurred to me as I sat in the middle of all of this that the void I've been feeling lately was indeed a longing for my own kin and home folks.

As the celebration wound down and the well-wishers hugged goodbye, I wondered if maybe this closeness, this coming together, this nourishing of family ties is an essential ingredient for our contentment in later life.

I wondered if I'd still feel that unscratched itch if I'd taken more time to maintain those ties.

I wondered if, in fact, in this time of instant divorces and live-in arrangements, a 60-year marriage was an artifact of days gone by.

I wondered if, given our pace of life today, it were still possible for folks to live next to each other for decades, go to church and school together, neighbor with each other, raise kids together and grow old together as had this group of home folks in this little Oklahoma town.

I wondered if these folks knew something that my move-away generation didn't know about living a fulfilled and happy life, albeit a simple and uncomplicated one.

The answer, I think, was in their faces.

Their sweet, smiling Oklahoma faces.

It's Time for Airlines to Think About Consumers

July 25, 2002 : I don't know a cat-haired thing about running an airline. However, I honestly believe that any Wichita business-person could run one better than it appears the major ones are being run today.

Not long ago I had to fly to Nashville for a meeting. My travel agent booked the tickets two or three weeks in advance of the flight, and figured I was all set.

Not so fast, buster!

At the ticket counter, we were informed that we weren't confirmed from Wichita to St. Louis, but were confirmed from St. Louis to Nashville. "Gee," I said, using my best and shiniest smile, "We bought the ticket 2½ weeks ago."

The American flight attendant said something like, "We'll probably get you on OK, but this ticket has no seats assigned, and we are oversold on this flight."

Up went the anxiety level. "Gee," I said (I use that word a lot when I'm groveling), "what happens if we don't get on?"

"Well, then we'd put you on a later flight," she said with a nice smile.

What I didn't bother to tell her was that earlier I'd tried to change my ticket to that later flight and decided against it when I was told that it would cost a lot more, plus a cancellation fee of $125 per ticket.

Long story short, we did get on and in fact flew in first class to St. Louis because the cheap seats were oversold, but the first-class ones that cost more than a Kia automobile were mostly empty.

On the way back we encountered the same thing—no assigned seats from Nashville—and we were frostily notified that we were on standby, which in airline speak means "maybe you will and maybe you won't." (Not what you want to hear when you're coming home.) We didn't get to sit together, but we did get on yet another oversold plane.

When you read about how the airlines are losing money and needing government hand-outs to stay in business, you have to wonder what the heck is wrong. Here they are over-sold most of the time, charging an arm and a leg to make little changes, cramming us into those planes like a bunch of sardines and cutting overhead (such as meals), and still they say they're going broke.

Maybe what's needed is to rethink the concepts that most of the major airlines seem to apply to customers. As I said, I don't know much about running an airline, but here's what I'd do if I did run one.

1. I'd never oversell a plane. They have computers, for crying out loud. Surely they can tell when they're oversold.

2. I'd figure out what it costs to sell a seat at fair profit, and set that price regardless of when the ticket was bought. There would be no charge for merely changing flights. Some charge, maybe, for a last-minute cancellation if I couldn't sell the seat, but c'mon - it doesn't cost $125 to change a ticket.

3. I'd unplug the computer that does the yield-demand pricing that penalizes the customer who has to fly at the last minute. That policy is designed to stick it to you if you really need the airlines, and I can't believe it creates much customer loyalty.

4. I'd recognize that the indignities brought about by the necessity of stepped-up security have made flying a terrible hassle, and I'd try to make sure that my employees were trained to counterbalance that hassle with an attitude that would make Dale Carnegie smile.

5. I'd cut about five rows of seats out of a plane so people could get in a seat without bruising their chins with their knees.

6. I'd improve the baggage handling process so bags weren't destroyed or lost, then ban all carry-on luggage except purses, makeup bags and briefcases.

7. I'd rethink my policy toward travel agents, who perform a great service for the airlines for a small commission, and figure out how to work with them instead of trying to starve them out in favor of a Web site.

They haven't asked me, but if they did, in addition to the above, I'd advise the airline mucky-mucks to consider revising their attitudes and policies toward their customers so the skies were a little friendlier.

Maybe that would help forestall the need to ask Uncle Sam for a handout.

Country Music Needs to Get Back to Its Roots

BRAD PAISLEY, EDDIE ARNOLD & GARTH BROOKS CONGRATULATE
OL' MIKE ON HIS COUNTRY MUSIC ASSOCIATION'S PIONEER AWARD

AUGUST 8, 2002 : An old radio listener of mine came up to me the other day with a complaint. He said he'd all but turned off the radio because he couldn't stand to hear the stuff they're calling "country music" these days. He lamented the fact that his country music heroes, Merle Haggard, Johnny Cash, Willie Nelson, Patsy Cline and George Jones, were hardly ever heard on the air anymore.

He said the new "junk" (his word) was offensive to him. He said he misses the steel guitars and fiddles and harmonicas and mandolins and simple melodies that once defined what he termed real country music.

After he left I got to thinking about how many times over the last 40 years I've heard that same complaint.

I remember when the very artists he men-tioned were new and crowding the likes of Jim Reeves, Hank Locklin and Marty Robbins off the radio. That bunch pushed Red Foley, Lefty Frizzell and Webb Pearce off the radio. Before that, Lefty and Hank Williams and Carl Smith and their colleagues crowded the Carter Family, Bob Wills and Elton Britt off the airways.

In other words, country music reinvents itself about every 15 years with new art-ists and new sounds. It evolves. Just as pop music, jazz, and rock change with the passing decades, so does country music.

The trouble with all that is that each evolution leaves some of us behind. We tend to define country music as what the style was when we became hooked on it. For me, the definition of "true" country music was the

93

Lefty and Hank era, the late '40s through the late '50s. Like my old listener, to me it ain't country if it doesn't have a steel guitar and fiddle in it.

However, to a twentysomething, the countryness of a song will forever be measured by the music of Garth Brooks and Tim McGraw and Reba McEntire, the generation that crowded Merle and Johnny and Willie and Waylon and their generation off the air.

One could easily argue that the reason country music has survived as a mainstream entertainment form is its ability to change with the times. Country artists often justify their forays into pop and rock music as a broadening of country music. The problem with that argument is that those style changes usually result in music that is neither fish nor fowl. It's not really country, and at best is bad rock or pop.

Country radio station programmers have pushed the envelope also, using the same broadening justification, usually with bad results. They tend to alienate the "true" country listener and fail to attract the listener who can't stand any country.

This general attitude, by the way, led most so-called country stations to totally overlook the most recent trend-setting event in music, the emergence of the "O Brother, Where Art Thou?" soundtrack, which is composed of hard-core, old-time bluegrass music.

That exquisite form of snobbery probably cost country stations an audience, as the listeners turned to their own CD players and public radio, which has been playing the soundtrack.

My old listener and the others who feel as he does, the "true" country music fans, can take comfort from the fact that the music will return. Because it is a commercial industry, the record companies and radio stations can no longer afford to ignore the success of the "O Brother" soundtrack and the continuing success of pure country artists like George Strait and Alan Jackson.

You watch. A whole trend will appear soon, and the copycats that rule the industry will fall over themselves to get on the "O Brother" bandwagon. Artists and record companies and stations that have been too uppity to give us plain, simple, unhomogenized country music will get back to their roots.

Just as it did a decade and a half ago when the likes of Randy Travis, the Judds, Ricky Skaggs and others ushered in the last round of neotraditionalism, the industry will realize that it once again has gone too far and will return to dance with the one that brung it.

That would make a lot of folks like my old, disenfranchised listener (and me) mighty happy.

Enthusiasm Can Unlock the Door to the Good Life

AUGUST 15, 2002 : A young man who waited on me in a place of business the other day had the personality of a parking meter.

This kid was the most unenthusiastic person I've encountered in years. I resisted the urge to lecture him on the attributes of enthusiasm, but I can't deny that I had the urge to set him straight. He seemed like a smart young adult, reasonably good looking and neat, but, boy, could he use a dose of good old-fashioned enthusiasm.

OK. Maybe I'm just not with it anymore, but I believe enthusiasm is just about one of the most important qualities anyone, let alone employees, can have. Enthusiasm is the mortar that holds the bricks of our lives in place.

Think about the people you know who are the opposite of enthusiastic. Do you like to be around pessimists? Now think about the folks you know who are bubbling over with enthusiasm. They see good in most everything they encounter, and they approach even the dullest of tasks with a great zest that belies failure. Those are the people you like to be around. Those are the people who inspire you, challenge you and make you want to do everything better.

Unfortunately, it's considered cool these days to act un-enthusiastic. It's a style statement to be unflappable and nonchalant about most everything. Ask your teenager about whether he or she is excited about something, and you're likely to get a "whatever" and a yawn. In the workplace, employees who are outwardly enthusiastic are considered to be gung-ho dorks or, worse, are said to be kissing up to the boss.

Well, at the risk of being totally uncool, let me tell you why I think enthusiasm is so valuable.

1. Enthusiasm fuels energy. Show me an enthusiastic individual, and I'll show you a person with seemingly boundless energy. The ones I've been around get more done in a day than some do in a week. They definitely accomplish more of their goals and, I'd wager, struggle less.

2. Enthusiasm breeds success. Most of the successful business people I know have an unbridled enthusiasm for their profession. They live it, eat it, breathe it and talk about it with a sparkle in their eyes that just says, "What I'm doing is the most fun in the universe!" Most of the folks I know who are successful at just being a good person are enthusiastic about their kids, their friends, their community and their lives in general.

3. Enthusiasm promotes good health. I really believe that the body is kept well by an enthusiastic outlook. I know a lot of people who could have easily been soured by health problems, but somehow through their enthusiasm for living they were able to ward off the illness that plagued them. I don't believe it can cure all illness, but enthusiasm can certainly help us deal with the maladies of man and make for a better quality of life.

4. Enthusiasm is an acquirable trait. Many of our attributes, or lack thereof, are the results of things over which we have no control. A talent for singing, or athletic abil-

ity, or physical appearance, for instance. But if you are unenthusiastic about things, you can change your outlook by simply willing it.

By looking for the reasons to be enthusiastic rather than the reasons not to be, you will become enthusiastic. It really is that simple! Once you start the process, you'll have the power to at least become competent at those attributes like singing and athletics. As for physical appearance, an enthusiastic person is always more attractive than an unenthusiastic one!

Heck. I'm no psychologist, but I'll take enthusiasm over all the other qualities, in kids, employees and friends.

I kind of wish I'd taken a moment to at least tell that young man how he was coming across. It probably wouldn't have made much difference, and I might have gotten a "whatever," but in case he's reading this, let me just say: Kid, for both our sakes, and for your employer's too, get enthusiastic, will you?

The World Is Full of Things That Make Me Nervous

August 22, 2002 : You don't hear the term nervous breakdown much anymore. Fact is, I never was too sure what that meant anyway.

Old Missus Hedgepath back in Marfa, Texas, where I was born, was said to have had a nervous breakdown after she caught her husband fooling around with his secretary, but I used to see her out in the yard and she looked OK to me. I mean, she looked kind of mad, but other than that she seemed perfectly normal. So I reasoned in those days that having a nervous breakdown wasn't all that fatal, just inconvenient, and that it gave folks something to talk about.

It wasn't until I got much older that I discovered that you could in fact get nervous about stuff to the point that it actually causes you to get sort of, you know, confused. Well, since I have noticed that I'm more confused about stuff the older I get, I'm beginning to get nervous about whether or not I'm getting nervous! I mean, today there are all kinds of things to be nervous about. I'll admit that some of 'em make me more nervous than a long-tailed tomcat in a room full of rocking chairs!

Take politicians, for instance. Those birds just plain make me nervous. They're shoveling money out the front door these days like there's no tomorrow, and pretty soon you and I will get the bill. Also, they're passing legislation that will dictate how our corporations will do business in the future. There's no question that some of these rogue companies need to be dealt with, but I'm not sure that Congress, given its record of fiscal murkiness, is the right entity to set the rules.

I don't know about you, but they haven't impressed me much with their ability to stay on top of their own financial matters, let alone Wall Street's. The fact that they've rushed in and started churning out more laws makes me nervous.

I'm also nervous about the West Nile virus. I don't know a cat-haired thing about it, but it must be bad because it's replaced forest fires as a main topic on the TV talk shows these days.

I'm nervous about that boy-band guy, Lance Bass, going up in space with the Russians. I'm not so worried about him going, but I'm pretty nervous about the fact that they may bring him back.

I'm nervous about the stock market. Just when you think it's going down, it goes up. When you think it's going up, it goes down. In the last couple of months it's been up and down more that a Duncan yo-yo. Just a couple of years ago we investors were trying to decide where to buy that second vacation home; nowadays we're trying to decide whether to go to work at Burger King or McDonald's to supplement our income.

I'm nervous that I might get arrested. See, I used to be a CEO before I retired, and since they have replaced drug dealers as the bad guys, I'm afraid that it's only a matter of time until they find out that I once was one and come and get me.

I'm nervous about political correctness run amok. The way I have it figured, by the year 2010 it will be impossible to do anything or say anything without offending some organized societal group.

There are a whole lot of other things that make me nervous. Driving on Rock Road, getting a colonoscopy, hip-hop music, Al Gore being resurrected, Krispy Kreme doughnuts (what if I get addicted?), Sam Donaldson's hair piece, El Nino (whatever the heck that is), bad cholesterol and myriad other things far too numerous to mention. So you can see, the older I get the more nervous I get.

Here's my question:

Do you think I'm on the verge of a nervous breakdown like old Missus Hedgepath?

Shared Grief of September 11th Changed Us, United Us

SEPTEMBER 5, 2002 : Back in the '70s, University of Colorado professor Morris Massy attracted some notoriety with a presentation he called "What you are now is where you were when."

Massy made the point that generations are shaped by the significant emotional events that occur during their lifetimes.

He used the generations who lived through the Great Depression as an example, arguing that they were indelibly stamped with a fear of going into debt or living above their means because of the scars left by their common experience with economic disaster. He talked about how those who lived through World War II would remain patriotic for their lifetimes because of the profound patriotic fervor generated during the war.

He spoke of how the '50s imprinted those of us who lived through them with a commitment to morality, family and work, of how the '60s generation "tuned in and dropped out," and of how the differences in values between generations can make communication difficult.

Massy's lecture was designed to remind us that we must know where someone's values lie before we can communicate with them effectively.

He was also arguing that once we are imprinted with a set of values, that is pretty much it for the rest of our lives. We are not likely to change those values, he said, until we experience what he called "a significant emotional event." He also reasoned that a significantly large and emotional event, such as the Depression, World War II and John F. Kennedy's assassination, could change an entire generation's values.

I think Massy was right on. Look at history. The carefree, partying "flapper" generation of the 1920s was changed to a fearful, cautious, desperate-to-survive generation by the Depression of the '30s.

That same generation, disillusioned by the government's handling of the economy, became our greatest patriots when we were attacked by Japan.

Ask anyone who experienced the Depression about the stock market, and they will tell you that it can crash and you'd better have some savings tucked away. Ask any World War II vet about how we should handle Iraq and he'll say "take 'em out" and do it thoroughly. Ask anyone what they were doing when Kennedy was shot, and they can tell you exactly where they were when the news broke.

Those events, most assuredly, were significantly emotional and changed the values of those generations.

You and I have now lived through another such event. Sept. 11, I believe, will prove to be the emotional moment of our time.

Entire generations were either not yet born or were too young to be affected by the Depression, the war or Kennedy's death and hence had no such significant emotional event to change their values. Now we have one.

As the anniversary approaches, we will again be reminded of our shared bond, of that awful day when we learned that our very existence is fragile and that the freedom we take for granted is not, after all, a given.

My generation is bound to those in generations before me who are still alive, as certainly as it is bound to my children and grandchildren's generations.

For each of our lifetimes, we will remember where we were and what we were doing when we first heard that a plane had crashed into the World Trade Center.

For each of our lifetimes, we will be indelibly changed: hopefully more appreciative of our freedom, more supportive of our leaders and military, and more aware of the precious gifts we have in our loved ones.

Maybe we were due. Maybe God allows mankind to cause a catastrophic event every few generations to make that significantly emotional impact on the untested generations.

To remind us.

Grandparents Hold a Store of Knowledge to Cherish

SEPTEMBER 12, 2002 : I found an old, faded photograph the other day in some stuff that had belonged to my mother. The picture was of a dark-haired young woman in a white blouse and dark skirt, seated at a counter with several other women.

The scene was obviously a telephone switchboard room, and the women were telephone operators at work. The equipment in the room tells you that it was taken a long time ago.

It took awhile, but I finally recognized the young girl in the foreground. It was my grandmother. She couldn't have been more than 18 or 19 when that picture was taken. As was the fashion in those old black-and-white photos, she wasn't smiling, just gazing at the camera like the other girls in the room.

When it dawned on me who she was, my mind traveled back to the last few years of her life, in her 90s. She would rock and talk to whoever would listen about how, as a young girl, she had traveled to St. Louis and worked for a time as a telephone operator. I didn't pay much attention to her memories then, but as I gazed at this old photo, I wished with all my heart that I had.

My grandmother's name was Ruth, but only my grandfather called her that. To all the rest of the family, she was "Ga-Ga," the closest I could come to saying grandmother when I was about 3. That name stuck, and she was Ga-Ga to all of us until she passed away at 95.

The Ga-Ga I knew and the girl in the photograph were as different as night and day. By the time I came along, she had married Floyd Nicholls, a feed store clerk who later in his life became treasurer of Presidio County, Texas, raised two sons and a daughter (my mom) and lost her firstborn in a drowning accident in Marfa, Texas. She was the mistress of a household that included her father, who was ill, my mom, me, my brother and sister, and her husband.

To supplement his meager income as treasurer and feed store clerk, they raised cows for milk, hogs for slaughter and chickens for eggs. She churned butter, tended a garden, baked pies and cakes, and did the washing.

Ga-Ga was the undisputed head of that household and could be as tough as she had to be. To this day, some 55 years later, I can remember the licking I got when, one afternoon, I thought the homemade bread she had baked would look better with holes punched in it, so I decorated the four loaves with my grubby little fingers.

She was also opinionated. Until her dying day she was a yellow-dog Democrat, and she believed until John F. Kennedy ran that Republicans and Catholics would be the country's ruin. She mellowed on Catholics because she liked JFK, but Republicans never received her absolution.

In her 80s, long after my grandfather had passed away, she ran a hotel and a restaurant and was the oldest Greyhound bus agent in Texas.

Staring at that photograph, I realized that there was so much about her life that I didn't know. She was willing in those last years to share it all, but I wasn't listening. She would recite stories from her long-ago for hours, and all I had to do was listen and ask questions and I would have inherited a century of knowledge that today would be priceless to me, but I wasn't listening.

Since I found that photo, I've been trying to remember the stories, the history and the relatives that she told of, and while I have retained some of it, I have lost so much more because I didn't listen as I wish I had. I wish

desperately that she were here to fill in the years between that serious young telephone operator and the apron-wearing, bespectacled, authoritarian grandmother who ruled the roost with an iron hand.

What was it like just after the turn of the last century, when she was a little girl? What was World War I like? The Depression? World War II? How did she deal with the death of her oldest son? All that history and wisdom was mine for the asking, and I let it slip away because I was too busy to listen.

It now seems like such a cruel joke that life plays on us. When we're young we're far too preoccupied with the things of the moment to pay attention to the old folks who have so much to tell. Then when we're finally old enough to appreciate what a treasure we have in our grandparents, they're gone, leaving behind a few fragmented memories and old, faded photographs that make us wish we'd been more attentive.

Photographs like the one of that serious and beautiful young operator who became my grandmother.

Here's to America's Truckers

September 19, 2002 : I just returned a couple of weeks ago from a motor-home trip to the Pacific Northwest. After logging nearly 3,500 miles in our coach, and traveling on four major interstates through seven different states, I came to the conclusion that truckers are cool.

I've always known it. After all, I made my living from country music for some forty years, and country music is rife with songs about truckers. "Truck Drivin' Sonofagun," "Six Days on the Road," "White Line Fever," "Phantom 309," "Looking at the World through a Windshield," and "Eighteen Wheels and a Dozen Roses" are just a few of the tribute songs to the breed of men women who make their living on this country's roadways.

Truckers, the serious ones, spend most of their lives keeping a 60,000- to 80,000-pound rig between the white lines, getting from point A to point B by the promised delivery time, They kiss their families goodbye, crawl behind the wheel of one of those monster rigs, and head for one of the coasts. They'll not come home again for two or three weeks. After one or two days home, they're off again.

Some have lost their families because of too many days away and too many missed Little League games. They typically don't belong to the Rotary Club or PTA or do any of the things that we consider "normal" because they have a run to make and a load that has to be there on time. They sleep in those cabs and Motel 6s across the country, when they do sleep. But sleep is secondary to getting to the next loading dock in time.

Truckers love truck-stop food, Merle Haggard, CBs with echo and linear amps, clean and shiny rigs, attractive and spunky truck stop waitresses, the latest Rand McNally map book, exit guides with big print, and holding court with their gear-pounding buddies at a Flying J truck stop.

They don't care much for rough right-hand lanes (after all, they pay enough taxes to keep them in good repair), weigh stations, smokies that lie in wait behind trees, company dispatchers, bad diesel, tough chicken-fried steak, Department of Transportation idiosyncrasies, liberal politicians or slow-running RVs.

But they are, in my opinion, the best drivers on the road, in general, they are the most courteous and most skilled vehicle operators on any interstate. Pass one and watch him blink his lights when it's safe to return to the right lane. Observe a car broken down along the highway, and if there's not a trucker parked behind to help, there will be soon. A lane change is always telegraphed by a signal. There are a few exceptions, I suppose, but you rarely see one exceeding the speed limit.

The CB is a trucker's pipeline to sanity. Engage one in conversation on channel 19, and you'll find out anything you want to know about the weather ahead, the best fuel stop, the road repair and where the next rest stop is. That little handheld microphone is his version of the Internet, a cocktail party or a visit with a therapist.

Over the airwaves at 65 miles an hour, he can gripe, comment, joke, get advice and kibitz with his own kind. Listen awhile and you'll hear the heart and soul of the last American cowboy. You'll hear truckers' complaints, their troubles with the company, the bank and their relatives.

You'll hear their musings about the traffic they encounter, their funny stories and their thoughts about the government. And you'll hear it in an accent that can only be described as "trucker-ese." It's a combination of a Southern and Western drawl unique to truckers, no matter where they come from.

An acquaintance of mine was griping about the number of trucks on the interstate the other day, and I thought to myself that without truckers there wouldn't be any interstate. Furthermore, a trucker hauled in most of the food my friend eats, most of the clothes he wears and most other goods that he depends upon- all because of a diesel-smelling, ballcap-wearing, CB talking, rig-running, smokey-dodging, taxpaying, flag-waving trucker.

So here's to 'em. May their engines run smooth, their hauls be short and their weight be legal. And may we always remember that the wheels of the economy we depend on total 18.

No Matter How Much We Own, We're Renters

SEPTEMBER 26, 2002 : The older you get, I guess, the more you start contemplating the meaning of life. You don't think about it much until you wake up one day and realize that you've probably passed the halfway mark in your tenure on this earth and it's all downhill the rest of the way. You become reflective. You begin to take stock of what you've accomplished with your years. You begin to question what legacy you will leave.

Will those you leave behind remember you? Will your memory be sweet to them, or will it be bittersweet? Will you still be on their minds years after your departure, or will they forget you days after they lay your bones to rest?

I recently had a bout of that kind of pondering while returning from that lengthy motor home trip to the Northwest that I mentioned last week. (There's not much else to do behind the wheel of a motor home, rolling down the interstate, but to ponder.)

Anyway, as I was grappling with the sweet mysteries of life and counting my material blessings, a powerful thought occurred to me.

It was . . . are you ready?

When it comes to the material things of this world, we are all just renting. That's right. We don't really own anything. We call it owning, and we spend our lives acquiring ownership of homes, cars, businesses, land, etc., but we don't really own any of it. We just use it for a while.

We accumulate stuff and, too often, I think, tend to measure our life's worth by how much stuff we have collected.

Many of the things that we work so hard to accumulate are in our possession for only a short time. Cars, hot tubs, swimming pools, clothes, gadgets all wear out and are traded or junked after use. Houses and land and businesses are sold to pay for the assisted-living facility that will warehouse us until we "meet our maker," as they used to say in Texas, or are bequeathed to our kids, who most likely will dispose of them sooner or later.

In a few short decades after death, even the deepest footprints are erased and life goes on, and the stuff we strove so hard for either rusts away or passes on to another renter. Another way to think of it is that, in a couple of hundred years, your house may be a parking lot, or under a reservoir, or under the paved streets of a future metropolis, just like the buildings of the old settlement that began Wichita.

Open an old magazine from the '20s and see who the big shots were then. Ask yourself how many of them you remember, or have ever even heard of. Yet they were as pertinent and relative to those times as we are in our respective turfs now. The issues that caused those people to burn with passion and energy are now cold embers long forgotten, just as the issues of today will be in 100 years to those who come after us.

The conclusion I came to somewhere out on I-70, dear reader, is this: We are all just renting. We are all temporary. At least here on this earth. The phrase "ashes to ashes, and dust to dust" fits all things, and all things will become one or the other in time.

What the heck is the real meaning of life, then? If everything is temporary and if all our efforts to fortify our immortality with material goods are futile, why did God even bother to put us here? I'm not the guy to answer that, but here's a clue where to seek the answer.

Go see your pastor or priest or rabbi.

The one thing that has endured all these centuries is mankind's belief in a hereafter. That idea has outlasted all the empires, all the kings, all the wealthy accumulators and all the challenges to its authenticity through the ages.

Maybe, like the old spiritual says, we are all just passing through, and the ownership we seek lies not in accumulation of stuff but in how we choose to treat our friends, our families and our neighbors.

Maybe this life is but a small part of the journey, and we should acquire character and compassion as well as material stuff.

Don't misunderstand me. I don't think there's anything wrong with accumulation as long as we remember that it isn't permanent and we're only renting it for a while.

A character that is defined by compassion, love and kindness toward all living things might be our only chance at being remembered more than a few weeks after the funeral.

We might be able to own that.

Wichita Exec Latest Victim of Corporate Inhumanity

OCTOBER 3, 2002 : The recent, abrupt discharge of KSNW Channel 3 General Manager Al Buch by the station's corporate owners left me a bit unnerved. It was yet another reminder that the incorporation of America, and more specifically our hometown of Wichita, has a cold and unfeeling side. It is yet another reminder that corporations lack souls.

Corporations, large ones anyway, apparently are incapable of showing loyalty to, and preserving the dignity of, those who serve them. Don't get me wrong. I believe strongly that a company has every right to assess its employees' contributions and change its personnel as it sees fit to enhance or protect its investment. I also recognize that when a new owner comes to town, change is inevitable.

It's the way they do it that bothers me. Cold. Impersonal. Sudden.

Al Buch was quoted as saying he didn't see it coming. His story isn't that different from those of other former executives and employees around town who became road kill along the highway of corporate takeovers.

Aside from the inhumanity of suddenly depriving a person of his or her livelihood, it's just plain stupid. It's stupid because it scares the remaining employees, who inevitably wonder who's next when they see a person they've come to know and be comfortable with discharged in such a heavy-handed way.

In the case of upper-management executions, it's stupid because unless the manager was incompetent, he or she has probably endeared himself or herself to the community. More important, he or she has likely gained valuable insights into the community that could help a new executive trying to get up to speed. When the old leader is summarily dismissed and marched out the door, the new leader has to start all over, and it can take years just to get back to even.

I wonder why corporations don't get it. Employee experience and morale, and community image, are many times the only real advantage the acquired company has over its competitors. When that presence goes out the door with the employees' boxed-up possessions, it is sometimes irretrievable.

To my admittedly simple country way of thinking, it would be far more intelligent for the acquiring corporation to have a more gradual succession from the old to the new. Bring the new horse in, plan a dignified exit for the old horse, and give the old horse the responsibility of showing the new horse around the barn.

In the absence of incompetence or dishonesty, it would seem to me that that kind of transition would be far less expensive than the macho slash-and-cut technique that prevails in so many of today's takeovers. Of course, it depends on the exiting employees' willingness to participate.

I've heard corporations justify their actions by bragging that they granted their amputees outplacement services and generous severance packages. I doubt, however, that those so-called benefits compensate for the loss of the dignity and security earned by years of service.

I reckon I'm not in a position to second guess the actions of companies that invest millions in acquisitions. But it's pretty easy to track the loss of community relationships by the big guys who've pounced on successful Wichita businesses and failed to calculate the worth of the stable, loyal employees who built the business.

I don't know if the big companies will ever be capable of determining the asset value of employee longevity, loyalty and experience in the companies they acquire. But I fervently believe that if they don't figure it out, they'll get their corporate heads handed to them by the competitors who do.

In my outsider-looking-in opinion, Al Buch was a good horse. He was the consummate broadcaster and did a great job of involving Channel 3 in the community. He served on several boards, volunteering his time and the station's to the extent that he was easily the most visible media general manager in town.

During his 15 years or so in Wichita, he survived several corporate owners, adapting to their cultures and shepherding their investment with dignity and skill. It just seems that his departure could have been handled differently.

But then, what do I know?

It's Never Too Late to Reunite with Estranged Parents

OCTOBER 17, 2002 : Dear readers: I'm aware that many family estrangements are not the fault of the children but are in fact caused by dysfunctional parents. This column isn't intended to address those situations today. This is about those who've become alienated from their parents because of family disagreements.

I know a lady who may be one of the sweetest and most generous people in our community. She has a warm and loving heart that manifests itself in a smile that could light up the Coliseum. She has an untold number of friends who think she's an angel on earth.

In all the years I've known her, I've never heard her say an unkind word. I could list countless good deeds she's done without asking for anything in return, and I'm sure I don't know the half of it. When you encounter her, you are instantly aware of her twinkling eyes and her sunny outlook on life.

However, she hides a profound sadness. I don't remember how it came up, but she confessed to me one day that her biggest disappointment in the autumn of her life is her estrangement from one of her children. This child has chosen to disassociate from the family and apparently harbors resentment and bitterness that mystify my friend.

Her letters to her offspring go unanswered. She hears news of her child from time to time but has had no direct contact for some while now.

As she spoke to me about the situation, that happy, angelic countenance turned sad and bewildered. Her eyes misted over as she told of the pain and emptiness and concern she feels almost daily now, knowing that one of her own is so resentful and alienated and distant, and not knowing why.

I'd seen that deep, despairing look before. I saw it on the face of my grandmother, whose youngest son drifted away from the family and never bothered to contact her for the last 30 years of her life. She grieved all of those years at his absence and finally convinced herself that he must be dead or, surely, he would have written. He turned up a couple of years after her death, alive and well.

I'm sure that these incidents are just two of many. Lots of families, it seems, have a black sheep or prodigal child who punishes his or her parents by disappearing, denying them what all parents must do to be fulfilled: witness their children growing and maturing. It's the ultimate form of punishment.

"I'm mad at you, so I'll deny you my presence" seems to be the motivation for many, but for others - as in the case of my long-lost uncle - I suspect it's an emotional defect, a lack of consideration or a void of human concern for those who gave them birth. Regardless of the reasons, the result is the same. The parents, like my friend, find it a wound that cannot be healed, a chasm that cannot be bridged and a burden that cannot be lifted.

The irony for the wayward sons and daughters is this: Unless they overcome their anger and resentment or lack of caring while their parents are alive, they are doomed to live under a cloud of self-loathing and regret for the rest of their lives.

One day, you see, they will be called to a bedside in some hospital and watch helplessly as their mother or father slips away. Or a phone will ring in the middle of the night with the news that Mom passed away yesterday.

Tears of regret will undoubtedly follow in all but the most hardened of these prodigal misfits, but it will be too late. Too late for forgiveness, too late for reconciliation, too late to reverse the course of events that caused so much hurt to those who loved them no matter what.

If I could, I'd tell every one of these prodigals to forgive and forget. I'd tell them that no disagreement is worth the angst and heartache that clouds their lives. I'd tell them to go immediately to the feet of their parents and beg forgiveness for the lost months and years and the terrible pain their absence has caused.

I'd tell them to go now.

Before more time is lost.

Before it's too late.

An Ode to a Trusted Companion Long Gone

OCTOBER 24, 2002 : He was ragged and matted with mud, and his black-and-white coat was covered with burrs when I first saw him that day in front of the radio station.

The receptionist said that there was this poor, hungry-looking dog hanging around, and I went to see. He was out on the front lawn, holding a piece of torn paper in his mouth. I tried to get him to come to me, but he was far too wary of humans by now to trust any of us, let alone a country disc jockey wearing a suit and tie and cowboy boots.

He just stared at me, holding the piece of paper and keeping his distance. He sniffed at me once or twice, then disappeared around the corner, and I figured we'd seen the last of him.

Next morning, though, he was back. (The receptionist had put a little pan of water and some sandwich leftovers out, and I reckoned he was checking for more.) I again tried to lure him to me, but he was just as standoffish as he'd been the day before.

He would turn up every day or two for the next couple of weeks, staring at me as I entered the building with a look that seemed to indicate that he was measuring me, sizing me up, deciding whether to trust me.

Then, one morning at 5:00, we became friends. He was waiting for me in my parking space at the station, came to me as I got out of the car, licked my hand and padded in behind me as I walked into the building.

I fed him some coffee cake, which he accepted gratefully, and went on the air as he found a comfortable spot underneath the broadcast console where I did my work. I took him home that night, and under protest from my sweet wife (we already had two dogs), he spent the night in the garage.

Next morning, he was sitting on the hood of my car when I got ready to leave, hopped in the back seat when I opened the door and took up his same sleeping place in the control room when we got to the station.

I broadcast his description over the air for the next few days and, I'm not ashamed to say, was relieved when no owner turned up. For he had quickly become my dog. A listener suggested the name Traveler, for after all, hadn't he traveled into my heart and home?

My wife relented after only a day or so. I suspect she knew we'd have to get rid of me if we couldn't keep my newfound companion.

In the years that followed — 15, I think — Traveler and I were inseparable. He went everywhere I went. To work, to meetings, on trips to our other stations, to concerts, to parties. When we'd get to wherever we were headed, he'd find a place in the corner of the room and watch the proceedings with perked-up ears and alert eyes that made clear to all that he was focused on his master and wasn't about to let me out of his sight.

He played soccer with our boys and the neighborhood kids and was the best goalie they had. He went down the road every morning to retrieve the paper and dutifully brought it to the front porch. He lived to be let out of the car a block or two from the house when we came home in the evening, to race me home.

I swear that he understood English. Once, Channel 12 did a story on his habit of racing to the front door of the station for a treat whenever the receptionist would announce on the P.A. that the "lunch truck is here."

He had his own jingle on my radio show, and when it would play, he'd howl along, harmonizing with the singers. In time, he got more fan mail than I did, and I'm certain he was a far bigger personality with our listeners.

More than 10 years have passed since my son and I buried my old companion in the front yard, in a pouring rain after old age claimed him, and still I think of him daily. In many ways, he was the best friend I ever knew.

His successor dogs, Ranger and Dyna, are likewise wonderful companions, but I suppose I'll always have a place reserved in my heart and mind for Ol' Traveler. Some days lately, when I'm driving home, I can see him running like the wind alongside the car, trying to beat me home, or coming up the road with the newspaper in his mouth, or running with the soccer ball, a pack of kids chasing him.

I know not the words to express how much I miss that dog or how much he meant to me. But I do know that I'm so very fortunate that, for all too brief of a time in my life, he was my companion.

My warm, trusting, loyal, intelligent companion.

Dad Feels Helpless as His Youngest Heads to KC

OCTOBER 31, 2002: Dear Kansas City, Mo.: You've pretty much torn your britches with me. I used to like you a lot. You were a fun place to visit, shopping in your stores was a great experience, and I did a lot of business in your downtown when I was running a company. But now you're on my list.

You're claiming my youngest son, my daughter-in-law and my grandbabies. My son has accepted a job with one of your radio stations and will soon leave Wichita to seek his fortune in your marketplace. He's excited and thrilled at his new opportunity, and I admit to being proud for him and the pos-

sibilities that his new position offers him and his little family.

I also admit to being depressed.

You see, he's my youngest. He's the last of the little birds to fly the nest. His sister and brother have already moved away to find their own pathways, and now he will, too. Instead of being three minutes away, he will be three hours away. Oh, we'll see each other, but it will be harder and harder. He'll be busy at his new job, and his old father will be less and less important to him as he makes his mark on his own.

I know that's the way it's supposed to be, the way it has always been, the way it was with me many years ago, but it's still depressing. I don't blame you, Kansas City, for that. But I will blame you if your big-city ways change my kid.

You see, to me he's still the same little 4-year-old frozen in that photograph his mother snapped so many years ago - wearing a coonskin cap, leaning on a toy rifle, gazing out across the back yard. He's still the little kid holding my hand as we walked along an aspen-lined path in Colorado on that long-ago vacation, peppering me with questions about the trout we were sure we'd soon catch, again captured by his mother's camera.

He's still the stoic young man holding back tears at his mom's funeral, being strong for his brother and sister and dad, but with a quivering lip that shined a spotlight on his sorrow. Though he's well in to adult-hood now, he's still idealistic and pure in his beliefs, still wants to be a great father and husband, still is optimistic and upbeat.

You change that, make him cynical or tough or disappoint him, and you bet I'll blame you!

His sweet wife believes her responsibilities as a mother take precedence over all else, and she spends her waking hours smoothing the path for her three little girls, giving them the love and attention that will make them always know they are important and valued. She was able to do that unencumbered in Wichita. If you place obstacles in her path and make her life harder, I'll blame you.

My little granddaughters are as innocent and sweet as God intended them to be. They are trusting and sincere, they feel safe and secure, and they approach every day with wide-eyed curiosity. They are not smart-mouthed or destructive or inconsiderate. They mind their parents and respect other adults. You change them one iota, and believe me, I'll blame you.

Look here, Kansas City. I know I'm not the first father to see his offspring move away to your neighborhoods and fancy restaurants and shopping centers, but right now, I feel like I am. I know that this hole in my heart will gradually heal, as it did after first his brother, then his sister, moved away, searching for new challenges. They survived, and I suppose he will, too. It's just that he's the youngest, you know.

I confess that his living just around the corner gave me the wherewithal to cling to the threads of what was once our way of life. He's the last vestige of that life together, and his leaving changes everything forever. We'll still be a family, we'll still be together on special days, but you, Kansas City, will shape the attitudes and outlooks of my youngest son, daughter-in-law and grandbabies more than I will.

They come to you from a community that has engulfed them in warmth, nurtured them and kept them safe up to now. They come to you full of hope and excitement. They come to you happily, with great anticipation for your wonder and quality of life. They come to you still impressionable and innocent.

Please, Kansas City, don't let them down. Don't make me have to come up there!

~ Ol' Mike.

More Might Run for Office If They Knew How

NOVEMBER 7, 2002 : I heard a fellow talking the other day about what a shame it is that more qualified folks don't enter politics. He was lamenting how, in his opinion, the crop of candidates for a particular office didn't seem to be the sharpest blades in the knife, and wondering why the office didn't seem to attract many qualified candidates.

Well, sir, I got to thinking about that poor fellow's concern, and it dawned on me that here was an opportunity for this column to do yet another public service.

Yes, dear reader, after observing several political campaigns, I've prepared a "how to be a politician" checklist that should, when followed, prepare more candidates to enter the political life in pursuit of your votes.

1. Pick an office that looks easy. You want to kind of slide into this thing, starting with an office that no one pays much attention to. Dog catcher or precinct commissioner or governor might be a few suggestions.

2. Hold a news conference and announce that you are running because you believe in a "better America" and your family and friends have urged you to bring your talents to the job. Be sure to emphasize that you will run a positive campaign on the issues and won't say anything negative about your unqualified opponent.

3. Hit up all your friends for money. Send them a letter that starts with, "Together we can make a difference," and ends with, "We're counting on you."

4. Get one of your friends to be your campaign chairperson, preferably someone who has some prominence and some friends with money.

5. Hire one of those political consultants to do polls for your campaign. It's better if you wait for the polls to be conducted before you commit to a position on anything, so you'll be sure to have a position that is popular with the voters.

6. Order 50,000 blue and yellow or red, white and blue yard signs. Have them put up everywhere, particularly in your opponent's neighborhood.

7. Hold a news conference and announce that your polls show that your positions are favored by a vast majority, and that your no-good opponent's negative attacks on you are not going to play well with the public and that you refuse to sink to his (or her) level.

8. Send a new letter to your friends that starts with, "When we got into this race we didn't realize how much it would cost to get our message out," and ends with, "(insert spouse's name) and I really need your support."

9. Have your campaign manager organize a $1,000-a-plate dinner for 300 or 400 of your closest friends and serve them a $2.29 chicken dinner. At that dinner, let them know that the fight has "only just begun."

10. Have the political consultants make a TV commercial that contains shots of you: hard at work at your desk; listening intently to a bunch of workers or, if possible, firemen; walking in a wheatfield with a farmer with your sleeves rolled up; and playing in the front yard with your kids. (If you don't have

any kids, borrow the neighbors' baby and hold it up in the air. Make sure the voice-over announcer has a low, quiet, reassuring voice and intones that your election will ensure a better future.)

11. Hold a news conference and announce that you've tried to run a positive campaign, but your no-good, lying, skunk-faced opponent keeps slinging mud, and challenge the low-life to a debate on the issues.

12. Send a letter to your past contributors that begins with, "My opponent is outspending me with negative attacks, and I desperately need your help to counter his outright lies with the truth!" Close with, "If you don't step up to plate, we may not realize our dream of a better America!"

13. Run a TV ad that takes the gloves off and accuses your no-good, gizzard-headed, frog-breathed opponent of lying about your record and running a negative campaign.

You know, after looking this checklist over, I think it just dawned on me why more people ain't running for office these days!

We Could Learn Plenty from Elderly, If We'd Listen

NOVEMBER 21, 2002 : Back in Marfa, Texas, where I was born, way before political correctness became a national epidemic, we called them "old folks."

The term was applied to our older aunts and uncles, grandparents and neighbors who had reached certain maturity. It was a term of utmost respect, applied to those who had earned their wrinkles and graying hair by weathering the storms and assaults of a sparse life in a sparse west Texas town.

Old folks had the right-of-way in our little town. No one honked at them when they lingered at the stop sign or complained that they took too much time at the grocery store counter. No one fussed about having to care for relatives who had become old folks. It seems to me now that almost every family I knew had old folks living in their home.

You see, there weren't any assisted living or nursing homes in which to warehouse the old folks. They lived independently in their own homes until they could no longer fend for themselves; then they moved in with their sons and daughters or brothers and sisters and occupied the exalted position of old folks until they passed on.

I admit to being too young at the time to really be in the know, but I don't recall hearing anyone ever gripe about having to care for the old folks. It was pretty much a given that home care was the expected.

One of my earliest memories is of my grandmother's father, who lived with us until he died in his bed, in his room. We, of course, lived in my grandmother's house, and for a time, while great-granddaddy was alive, four generations lived under that one roof. It just seemed like the natural order of things.

I mention it because I think that as a society we are wasting a vast and wonderful resource in our old folks.

No, I'm not saying that it's wrong for our old folks to live in assisted living and nursing homes. Yes, I know how beneficial it is for them to be in the company of their contemporaries in a planned retirement center, and of course I'm aware that given today's pace and pressure it is simply not possible for all families have the old folks move in.

It just seems that so much is lost when we can't spend time with the old folks like we could if they lived with us.

Old folks know things that we need to know. Old folks have experience in the ups and downs of life and want nothing more than to share it with someone they love. Old folks long for precious time with their kin. They hunger for news of loved ones' accomplishments, and they long to tell their stories to their children and grandchildren before they leave this earth. So they'll know. So they'll have a history to relate to their children.

Old folks are wise. The wisdom that is so needed in this world by those of us who will be old folks (if we're lucky) is there for the taking, but too often we ignore it or, worse, don't even make the time to listen to it.

Most of the old folks I know are patient and thoughtful and kind. They are patriotic. They are generous and understanding. They have knowledge that transcends years and have already tread the paths that we who come after them will have to navigate.

They've fought wars, and survived economic disasters and illness and sadness and sorrows on their way to becoming old folks.

How tragic it is that we don't listen to them more. Learn from them. Visit with them. Respect them. How vast is the lost wisdom and experience. How truly tragic. I know the politically correct terms. Senior citizens. Seniors. Mature adults. To me, they will always be old folks. The old folks who built the cities, wrote the laws and paved the way for the blessed life I am enjoying.

I saw a couple of old folks walking down the street downtown the other day. He was dressed in a suit and tie and wore an Irish-type field cap; she had on a flowered dress and hat and carried a purse. They were arm in arm and walking slowly and deliberately toward the church.

He steadied her as she stepped off the curb; then she did the same for him. Then, hand in hand, they crossed the street and began the climb up the stairs to the Lord's house, no doubt for their weekly visit.

I reckon He listens to the old folks.

Jack Jonas' Vision Was Dignity for the Disabled

DECEMBER 5, 2002 : I watched Vern Houchin work for nearly 15 minutes. He was inserting number templates into a press machine, stamping out Kansas license plates, one number at a time so the sequence would be right.

Each number was on a different template and had to be inserted at just the right time, then quickly removed and placed back in line while the next number was snatched from the line and inserted in the machine.

Vern worked with the quickness and dexterity of a cat, his right hand doing something different from his left in a rhythm that was almost musical in its cadence. Occasionally, without slowing down or losing his place, he'd look over his shoulder and smile at us as we watched.

It was a smile of pride. A smile that said, "I'm doing something here that no one else can do as well as me."

He beamed as Walt Aikman, president of Center Industries Corp. (CIC), explained that what Vern was doing for several hours a day was impossible for Walt to do well for more than a few minutes.

Vern, you see, has a disability. He and about 125 other disabled Wichitans work at CIC. They make license plates for Kansas and several other states; they do manufacturing work for Boeing, Rubbermaid, Raytheon, Cessna, Bombardier, John Deere, Hayes Co. and the Department of Defense.

CIC began in 1975 as an affiliate to the Cerebral Palsy Research Foundation of Kansas, founded in 1972 by an amazing, far-sighted, tenacious little guy named Jack Jonas. Jack had a rather simple goal. He wanted to help folks with disabilities such as spina bifida; multiple sclerosis; mental retardation; head, spinal cord, and back injuries; hearing impairments and strokes lead a productive, economically rewarding and independent life. Quite simply, he wanted them to live with what most of us take for granted: dignity. The foundation's mission was to provide support for these folks with training, employment and technology.

See if you think he has succeeded. The $18 million foundation now oversees:
— Center Industries Corp., employing 170 people (75 percent with disabilities).
— The Daniel M. Carney Rehabilitation Engineering Center, which figures out how to re-engineer equipment so the disabled can use it.
— The Timbers, a 100-apartment complex for the disabled.
— The CPRF School of Adaptive Training, teaching digital technology skills to the disabled.
— The Mobile Rehabilitation Engineering Shop, a mobile shop that travels throughout Kansas, providing on-the-spot solutions to re-engineering problems.
— The Kenneth J. Wagnon Life Skills program and the K.T. Wiedemann Adult Learning Center, which assist adults in everything from physical therapy to arts and crafts.

The concept of re-engineering the workplace for the disabled has spread to other cities as more communities become aware of the foundation's example of how its clients can make superbly crafted products, live without taxpayers' charity and become proud taxpayers when given the chance. Jack retired a couple of weeks ago and handed the reins over to his son, Pat, who, along with Walt Aikman, derailed from his retirement by the pugnacious Jack, will run CIC.

You only have to look into the eyes of Vern and his co-workers to see the good that Jack, and all the people he has buttonholed to help, have done. Ask Jack who those enlistees are, and it's a who's who of politicians and Kansas entrepreneurs. He particularly praises former state legislator Pete Loux and Pizza Hut cofounder Dan Carney, the foundation's board chairman.

I can tell you that these people are true visionaries who epitomize the best that is in us mortals. They have addressed an age-old problem with good old-fashioned business sense and accomplished what seemed impossible a few years ago.

I do believe that Jack Jonas, the dynamic, "never take no for an answer" dreamer, and Dan Carney, the gentle, quiet, modest and unassuming benefactor of so many good things in this city, will be personally escorted to heaven when they leave this earth. Escorted, no doubt by a band of angels made up of the formerly disabled, given wings while still on earth by these two giants.

Ol' Mike's Holiday Joy Is Clouded
by More Bad Health News

JANUARY 9, 2003 : OK. Put me back on your prayer list.

By the time you read this, I hope to be lying on a gurney at M.D. Anderson Cancer Center in Houston, in one of those stupid little gowns with no back, being wheeled into a room where they can attack five or six little tumors they found in my liver.

Let me digress.

I went in for a regularly scheduled CT scan in mid-December. A couple of days later I got the call from Kansas Cancer Center informing me that "something was going on in the liver" and setting up a PET (positron emission tomography) scan the following week. The results showed there was definitely something going on.

The PET image is a more exact method of "lighting up" tumors. This scan confirmed what the CT scan had suggested: five small tumors. The doctor then ordered a liver biopsy, which we did immediately. The biopsy confirmed that the tumors were malignant, probably a carryover from my old bladder cancer problem back in January 2000.

Even though I had the operation that is supposed to contain cancer cells before they get out of the bladder, my doctor at Johns Hopkins tells me that in 20 percent of the cases some cells do get out and metastasize in other organs. (Now he tells me!)

Well, needless to say, all this news just before Christmas sort of put a damper on things around our house. I've been on the Internet for days trying to learn all I can about this latest stuff, while the kids and wife and friends have worried about me. My local doctor, who is very worried, suggested I get a second opinion at M.D. Anderson, and my records and tests have been sent. I hope, as I said, to be there when you read this.

You may be interested to know what I've found out so far:

There are two kinds of liver cancer: primary, which starts and resides in the liver, and secondary, from some other source (the kind I probably have).

Some cancers in the liver are treatable by resection (cutting part of the liver out). Mine probably won't qualify for that.

Liver cancer for the most part is treatable, but not curable yet.

Several treatment options are available that show promise, and maybe I'll be eligible for one or more of those. They include chemotherapy, radiation, a process in which they freeze the tumors, a process in which they kill the tumors with a heated probe, and an alcohol injection process that supposedly has promise.

Then there are the trials that are going on around the country that have possibilities, and a doctor in Italy who treated a 58-year-old man's liver cancer by removing the organ, radiating it with a nuclear device for 11 minutes, then reinstalling it in the patient. (He's alive and cancer-free after a year.)

As I write this, I don't have a clue about how they will treat me. I do know that we've caught these little tumors early, as they did not appear on my last CT scan 2½ months ago.

That may be the best chance I've got to get on top of this dad-gummed thing. Other than the mental aggravation that news like this creates, I'm as healthy as a horse, with none of the symptoms that usually show up with liver cancer. I figure I should be happy that I had lymphoma, which was discovered in August 2000 and, with the bladder cancer, caused me to get regular checkups.

And maybe the early detection and my overall good health will aid me in fighting this.

Heck, maybe when the second opinion arrives it'll be something simple, like gallstones or some danged infection. However, if the original diagnosis is correct, I'm mentally prepared to do battle with it. I, of course, will keep you posted.

For now, getting back on your prayer list would be appreciated.

Ol' Mike Offers a Prayer for All in the New Year

JANUARY 2, 2003 : Dear Lord, Your year of 2003 is upon us. Just like the last year, we begin it with new hopes and new dreams. We begin it full of confidence and certain that we can learn from the mistakes of the year gone by. We begin with a fresh optimism that somehow the days will be warmer and the sun will shine brighter and the world will be a better place. We begin with the knowledge that along with your help and guidance, it is up to each of us to make it so.

As for me, Lord, I plan to do my part. I've taken a look at myself in the context of the new year and find myself lacking in so many ways that I figure I'm in need of an overhaul! It occurs to me that there is no better time than right now, at the beginning of this new year, to start knocking those rough edges off and fixing the flaws that leap out at me every time I take inventory of my old carcass.

I haven't been very good at being humble this year. After my bouts last year with cancer, I got to feeling so doggoned good that I got kind of cocky. I felt 10 feet tall and bulletproof! I forgot for a while that every day I felt good was through your grace.

Well, now the doctor has discovered a problem in my dad-gummed liver, and I am instantly reminded of the fragility of this life and that it is you, not I, who holds the power over my good health. I am reminded that though I can participate in my own well-being by staying positive, eating right and exercising, it is your decision whether or not I get to be around for the next 35 years.

Therefore, I am resolved to deal with any new health challenge as best I can, but with the humble knowledge that how and if I get through it is in your hands.

I haven't been as thoughtful and kind to others as I wanted to be this last year. There's my uncle, whose son was killed in a car accident, who could have used more contact from me, and I didn't do as much as I could have done to comfort him. There are a couple of aunts who would have been cheered with a letter or a phone call that I didn't make. In short, I was so wrapped up in my own doings that I forgot to do my part to help brighten the life of some of those for whom I could have made a difference.

Therefore I am resolved to be kinder and more focused on what I can do for others, and less on what I can do for me.

I have, I'll admit, taken a lot for granted lately and perhaps have not been as thankful as I should have been for the abundant life you have given me. I look around and see wonderful children, angelic grandchildren, a sweet and loving wife, a full circle of great friends, a satisfactory and rewarding 45-year career, and a cup that truly overflows with your blessings.

I fear that too often I've complained about what I don't have and what bumps in the road I've encountered, and I have overlooked what you have provided and how you've helped me over those bumps. All too often I have readily accepted your gifts without the proper appreciation.

Therefore, I am resolved, as we begin this new year, to celebrate the life you have given me with a gratitude that is evident in all my speech, deeds and thoughts.

I'll have to confess, Lord, that I haven't always been the best at keeping my New Year's resolutions. I've found excuses to lay them by the wayside over the years, and in fact I've sometimes made them knowing full well that I wouldn't keep them.

But these are different. After 60 some-odd years on your earth, I reckon I'm finally getting closer to knocking on your gate.

When I do, I'd like my slate to be at least presentable so you can see your way clear to let me in. I'm not sure that even if I do keep these resolutions this next year it will be enough to overcome my past lack of attention to them, so if it's not too much to ask, I'd like a few more years down here to practice my good intentions.

I suppose it's a lot to ask, but I'll be grateful for whatever you can do.

Afterword

CROWSON'S VIEW

Reprinted from the *Wichita Eagle*

It was Christmas when Dad told us about the five spots they had found on his liver. "I've got to get a plan of attack ready and then I'll beat this thing," he tried to assure us, but he couldn't hide the fear in his eyes. Over the next two weeks he carried on with life, playing golf with friends and working on behalf of the city. All the while, he was rapidly educating himself on the available treatments for liver cancer.

After weighing the limited options, he narrowed his choice to two radical procedures: Extremely high doses of chemotherapy or the experimental approach that had been tried in Italy. The latter process involved removing the liver, treating it with radiation, then replacing it. He decided to go to Houston for chemotherapy, and save the trip overseas as a backup in case things didn't go as well as he hoped.

He arrived at the hospital just a few days later, ready to fight. But the doctors had devastating news. In a matter of days, the five spots had multiplied to five hundred.

It was Super Bowl Sunday when we got the call to come to Houston. We knew what this meant, but we still thought that the man that who had accomplished so much in his life, who had overcome so much during the last two years, might be able to win one more battle.

When we arrived and saw him there, with Pegi at his side, we weren't so sure. "Hey guys," Dad said in the best Ol' Mike voice he could work up. "We just hit a little setback here. We're gonna get the chemo going again and take care of this liver."

Judging by the look on Pegi's face, we knew that wasn't the case. But even that close to the end, Dad never gave up the stubborn optimism that had served him so well for 63 years.

For the next several hours we sat by his bed and got a chance to say a lot of important things to each other. He entrusted us to have this book of his beloved columns published because he wanted to share the important lessons that he'd learned over the last few years.

At one point, he was talking with Pegi and abruptly stopped in mid-sentence. Looking toward the door as if a new set of visitors had just stepped in, he asked, "Who are all these folks?"

Pegi didn't see a soul as she scanned the room. "What do you mean, Mike?" she replied.

"Can't you see all these folks who just came in?" he asked. When Pegi said she didn't see anyone, he responded, "Well, they must be angels!" As if nothing out of the ordinary had happened, he jumped right back into their conversation.

On Monday morning at 4:45, just like he did for 40 years while airing his radio show, Dad got a call. But this time it wasn't the overnight disc jockey phoning to tell him it was time to get up to come to the station.

It was God calling him home.